THE
Darden
Dilemma

Books by Ellis Cose

The Press
A Nation of Strangers
The Rage of a Privileged Class
A Man's World
Color-Blind

THE
Darden
Dilemma

12 Black Writers on Justice,
Race, and Conflicting Loyalties

EDITED BY ELLIS COSE

HarperPerennial
A Division of HarperCollinsPublishers

HarperCollins books may be purchased for educational, business, or sales promotional use. For information please write: Special Markets Department, HarperCollins Publishers, Inc., 10 East 53rd Street, New York, NY 10022.

FIRST EDITION

Designed by Elina D. Nudelman

Library of Congress Cataloging-in-Publication Data

The Darden dilemma : 12 black writers on justice, race, and conflicting loyalties / edited by Ellis Cose. — 1st ed.
    p.   cm.
  ISBN 0-06-095227-X
  1. Discrimination in criminal justice administration—United States.
2. United States—Race relations. 3. Darden, Christopher A.   I. Cose, Ellis.
KF9223.D37   1997
345. 73'05—dc21   96-46284

97 98 99 00 01 ❖/RRD 10 9 8 7 6 5 4 3 2 1

Before the O. J. Simpson trial, black prosecutors were all but invisible, toiling, for the most part, in various degrees of obscurity. Christopher Darden's front-and-center role in the so-called trial of the century brought them out of the shadows, but it did much more. The endless media coverage and Darden's subsequent best-selling book created a compelling and indelible portrait of the black prosecutor as a tortured soul—as a conflicted laborer in a perfidious place where celebrity, crime, and conflicting racial perceptions collide.

Darden's very selection as a Simpson prosecutor was rich with racial connotations—so much so that Darden felt it essential to establish early on, to his satisfaction at least, that his role was not primarily symbolic. "If I thought I was being named to the case primarily because I was black, I would've rejected it. It was as simple as that. But I knew that wasn't why I had been chosen." He was chosen, instead, Darden insisted, because he was good, because he knew the case, because he was available and willing. Nonetheless, in the eyes of his critics, such facts seemed irrelevant: "I was a black prosecutor, nothing more," he complained in *In Contempt*, as he responded to the pundits' reviews of his opening statement in the O. J. Simpson trial. "None of these armchair lawyers paid attention to the content of what I had said, only the pigmentation of my skin, the breadth of my nose, the thickness of my lips. 'Yes, he's black all right. That must be why he's up there.' Everything in this case was sifted through a filter of bigoted expectations, like the pressure Jackie

Robinson faced when he broke the color barrier in base-ball. 'Pretty good hitter for a darkie.'"

Darden's relationship with defense counsel Johnnie Cochran was no less defined by racial preoccupations: "Beneath the court case that everyone else saw, Cochran and I fought another battle, over the expectations and responsibilities of being a black man in America. He took shots at me . . . I listened with clinched jaw. Later, I began to fire back, to show there were responsibilities as a human being that were just as important as the responsi-bilities of being an African American."

Darden's inner turmoil was poignantly obvious during the trial as he wrestled with painful questions about the perception of his role. "Was I going to be seen as a brother putting another brother in jail?" Such issues, Darden con-cluded, would not keep him from the task at hand—or from the larger mission of opening up the justice system for blacks. "Perhaps I was naive, but I convinced myself that African Americans had to be represented in all seg-ments of the law if we were ever to believe that the sys-tem was ours too."

From the moment he decided to accept his appoint-ment to the case, Darden realized he could not afford to see himself as simply a prosecutor doing his job, for too many other people defined the role otherwise—and almost always racially. In some circles (usually white) he was seen as a principled, compassionate black tribune speaking out against racism among his fellow blacks. In other circles (generally black) he was viewed as a dusky

Judas, dispatched by a hostile white society to bring a strong black man down. He apparently saw himself as a man in the middle, caught between black and white racism, trying diligently to get jurors—and America—to focus on motive, opportunity, and evidence instead of race. By his own reckoning, he failed in that pursuit, largely, he believes, because of bigotry—or, as he put it, because the jury attempted to "defeat bigotry by cheating justice." The jurors, in other words (at least in Darden's estimation), rejected his view that they should play by the rules of the system to which Darden has dedicated much of his life. Darden's opinion about the jury is obviously disputable, and many of the contributors to this collection take issues with it. Still, his concern about the role of race in the justice system cannot be dismissed.

Since well before the dawn of the civil rights movement, black Americans have debated whether "the system" can be "ours too," whether America will ever fully honor its promise of freedom and justice for all. The nation's early history is not reassuring. There would have been no need, after all, for the Fourteenth and Fifteenth Amendments (intended to protect blacks against state persecution and discrimination), if authorities in many states had not been utterly hostile to the most basic notion of fairness for blacks. Though, in recent years, the concept of equality under the law has been widely accepted, the justice system in practice has not always lived up to that ideal. As Clarence Page makes clear in his essay in this collection, many blacks have sound reasons—

reasons rooted in personal experience—to distrust at least some aspects of the justice system. The shooting of a black motorist by a white police officer in St. Petersburg, Florida, in October 1996 and the riots that ensued in its wake reminded Americans, yet again, of why suspicions of the police (and the justice system they represent) refuse to disappear from America's black communities.

Darden concedes that "the system" harbors racial bias but suggests that, rather than defy or reject the system, blacks should strive to make it better. It makes little sense, in his mind, for blacks to "take themselves out of the justice system because it is sometimes unfair." If blacks are ever to have "real ownership in the system," Darden argues, principled and prominent black prosecutors are essential, for only through enforcing the laws can blacks really take ownership of them.

In the essays that follow, twelve (one is tempted to say, "a jury of") black thinkers grapple with various aspects of the "Darden Dilemma." The contributors differ, sometimes sharply, in their assessments of Darden—as a man and as a prosecutor. Stanley Crouch sees him as a whiner and as one who did a horrible job with the Simpson case and who yet, in the manner of George Armstrong Custer, has somehow emerged a hero. Marcia Ann Gillespie sees him as a naive soul. "It shouldn't take a jury acquittal to make a black district attorney face the fact that . . . an admittedly racist cop is a detriment to your case if the defendant is black."

Whatever their feelings about Darden, however, all the

contributors agree that, as Roger Wilkins puts it, he "had a tough job in a rough town," and a job made infinitely tougher by the mine fields of race. Darden himself equates the Darden Dilemma with the criticism black prosecutors get from other blacks for "standing up and convicting black criminals." Yet, more broadly defined, the dilemma is really about the pressures of being black in a society that has not always valued black life—and that continues to penalize black people for the color of their skin. As Elijah Anderson observes in the pages ahead, "simply being black poses a special problem of social, psychological, or even physical survival." Just to make it through the day, he argues, blacks pay a psychic tax: "Since the Rodney King beating, in particular, middle-class blacks, working-class blacks, and poor blacks often, and perhaps increasingly, agree on this point. As a young black man once told me, '. . . . When you see another black man get stopped by the police, you wonder how race figured into it. When you go into a store and the salespeople give you an extra bit of scrutiny, you wonder. When you're on the elevator in your apartment building and the elevator stops at a floor and the white woman waiting moves to another elevator, your first thought is race. Little things like that remind you as a black person that you are paying your black tax.'" And to make matters worse, America is imprisoning blacks (particularly black men) at a horrifying rate, in large measure because of drug laws that hit blacks with disproportionate force.

Former prosecutor Paul Butler is far from convinced

that Darden's faith is well-placed and in his searchingly candid contribution to this collection, he explains his pessimism. The Willie Horton incident, and others like it, believes Butler, establish "that it will be impossible for African Americans to achieve justice through traditional politics, including exercising their hard-gained franchise. Perhaps 'impossible' is too strong; it is better to say that it will take too long, and African Americans can't afford to wait, considering the emergency nature of the crisis. . . . If it took the white majority more than two hundred years to understand that slavery was wrong, and approximately one hundred years to realize that segregation was wrong (and still many don't understand), how long will it take them to perceive that American criminal justice is evil?"

Even many blacks who do not see American justice as evil do believe it has been and continues to be considerably less than fair. As Roger Wilkins observes: "There is no more important concept in American criminal law than the presumption of innocence. . . . Unfortunately, it still doesn't always work. In some places, poor, alienated black males are *presumed guilty*, not because of who they are as individuals, but because of where they are from, what they look like, and what their cultural affect is. In too many big cities, criminal justice is an ugly business. It is often carried on in battered courtrooms by overburdened and harried people. . . . However we Americans may have viewed the 'refuse of [somebody else's] teeming shore,' the refuse of America's poorest streets doesn't look very attractive to these overburdened people. The task of sorting out the individuality of surly, beaten, often defiant (and often guilty) people is sometimes beyond the capacities of the workers in this strained system."

According to a much-quoted analysis by a nonprofit Washington-based organization called the Sentencing Project, roughly a third of black men in their twenties are either in prison, in jail, on probation, or on parole. And the numbers, says the Sentencing Project, are virtually certain to get worse. Given that grim statistical reality, George Curry argues, "African Americans had more than ample reason to be suspicious of the criminal justice system as O. J. Simpson went on trial for murder. It was not that O. J. loomed large as an endearing figure among blacks—the *Pittsburgh Courier* sardonically noted that even his Ford Bronco was white—it was that African Americans continue to view the criminal justice system as a criminal injustice system." Inevitably that suspicion of the justice system colors how prosecutors (particularly nonwhite prosecutors) are perceived, and black prosecutors are acutely aware of their often suspect status. During an interview, Jeffrey Craig, deputy attorney general of Pennsylvania, confided, "Sometimes I'm very apprehensive about even telling black people what I do." The reason, as I explain in a separate essay, is that the information about his job often prevents people from seeing him for who he is: "[T]hough he prosecutes primarily white-collar crimes and most of his defendants are white, he knows that people won't recognize that fact from his job title. Nor will they understand that he is a critic of a system that, at times, especially when it deals with petty criminals, ends up 'putting a bandage on an infected sore.' The general public, he realizes, has no way of knowing that he goes out of his way to be fair to black defendants, that he shares many of the experiences they have had. . . . All his critics know, or think they know, said Craig, is that 'I'm a turncoat, that I'm not helping my brothers and sisters.' They see him, in short, as 'part of the assembly line of degradation and oppression of black people.'"

It is hardly surprising, in light of such sentiments, that black prosecutors sometimes feel conflicted. Nonetheless, Darden and many of his counterparts argue that they are doing the best they can with the hand that fate, circumstance, and the perpetrators' own actions have dealt them. "How could I put other brothers in jail?" Darden asked rhetorically and dramatically. "How could I not? As long as they were victimizing old people and making orphans of children, how could I not?"

Robert Grace, a young deputy district attorney in Los Angeles who was on the losing end of the 1996 murder prosecution of rapper Calvin Broadus (better known as Snoop Doggy Dogg), has made much the same argument. Grace bristled at Broadus's description of him as an "Uncle Tom." Broadus, he snorted, "had an entire table of white lawyers. And *he* talks about a sellout?"

At a meeting of fellow black prosecutors, Grace described a dinner with several black professionals at which the O. J. Simpson case was discussed. When it came to light that Grace was involved in the prosecution of Broadus, he noted, the atmosphere suddenly turned chilly. "Another brother trying to take another brother down," was one guest's description of his role. Grace was stunned. "Why," he asked himself, "are these people groaning at the fact that I'm involved in this case as an African American prosecutor?" Didn't they realize, he found himself asking, that the victim was a person of African descent? Didn't they know that people, black people, were dying of gun violence every day and that somebody needed to stand up and say, "This is wrong"?

From Grace's perspective—and from the perspective of many of his peers—getting killers (whatever their color) off the streets is a valuable, even essential, public service. "This is where I feel I can make the most difference every day," he said. And yet, he acknowledges (as a specialist in gang violence cases) that those he prosecutes are invariably black or Latino—a fact which serves as a disturbing reminder of the centrality of race on the streets and in the courts of Los Angeles.

In one of the most famous dissents in Supreme Court history, Justice John Marshall Harlan lectured his peers that the U.S. Constitution is "color-blind." "The destinies of the two races, in this country, are indissolubly linked together," asserted Harlan. In 1896, Harlan's colleagues on the Court were not prepared to accept such blasphemy, but in 1954 the Supreme Court reversed itself and granted blacks full equality under the law. Yet, in a country where blacks are roughly eight times as likely to end up in jail as whites, the very notion of color-blind justice is endangered, even if most of those blacks are guilty. Darden's dream of making the justice system "ours too" means little to defendants, or their families, who see that the only blacks present in any substantial numbers in court are those sitting in the docks. And as Andrea Ford, who covered the criminal court beat for the *Los Angeles Times*, reports, blacks in the court are not necessarily treated with respect: "I recall once almost colliding with two white police detectives at the entrance to the courthouse. After I slipped in ahead of them and walked toward the elevators, I heard someone behind me singing, "Hey, hey, she's a monkey," to the tune of the theme song of the old *Monkees* television show." When Ford turned she found the two cops smirking, causing her to wonder: "If this if the way they treated me . . . how did they treat the suspects they brought into court?"

Confronted with an overwhelmingly white structure and often with nasty attitudes as well, many blacks conclude, for obvious reasons, that there is more virtue in fighting such a system than in joining it, especially when that system seems hell-bent on putting huge segments of the black community under lock and key. As Butler puts it: "I know that one-third of my sisters and brothers are not dangerous or evil, and that any system of law that places them under its supervision is morally bankrupt and in need of immediate subversion."

In explaining the appeal of one of his fictional characters named Mouse (a stone-cold killer who "could gut a man and then sit down to a plate of spaghetti"), novelist

Walter Mosley observed: "For a group of oppressed people a man like Mouse is the greatest kind of hero. He's a
man who will stand up against bone-cracking odds with
absolute confidence. He's a man who won't accept even
the smallest insult. And for a people for whom insult is as
common as air, that's a man who will bring joy." Often,
added Mosely, "black men have to cross the white man's
rules because we know those rules never applied to us
anyway."

That sense of being excluded from and abused by the
system is pervasive in certain black neighborhoods. And it
is based not merely on theory but on painful personal
experiences. As Clarence Page relates in these pages, a
typical black response to an inquiry about the justice system would go something like: "*Sure, I know the system
doesn't work because my uncle got arrested and beat up by
the cops the other night and he ain't done nothin!*'"

Like Butler, Page parts company with Darden on the
issue of whether such experiences—and the anger and
resentments they create—interfere with the quest for justice in the courtroom. To the contrary, argues Page, those
resentments, in large part racial, enhance the integrity of
the judicial process by allowing real life to influence and
inform the proceeding of the court. History tells us,
argues Page, "that juries were created precisely to bring
values of the street to the courtroom"—even if that sometimes meant ignoring evidence and setting guilty defendants free as a means of passing judgment on the justice
process itself.

Page nonetheless worries that alienation from the system can sometimes be self-defeating. For it can not only lead jurors to reject evidence, but can lead people to reject a productive role in the larger society. It can lead young people, for instance, to dismiss book learning out of a mistaken notion that such a thing is "white" or to spurn mainstream jobs out of an untested belief that life in the white man's world will never be fair.

Yet, as Elijah Anderson argues, alienation among blacks—and certainly among black, inner-city youths—may be inevitable as long as America remains such a racially rancorous place. "Resigned to a society that does not include him in the American Dream," the young inner-city black man, writes Anderson, "comes of age realizing the hard truths that American society is not there for him, that a racially stratified system is in place, and that his place, fortified through acts of prejudice and discrimination, is at the bottom of it. This creates in him a profound sense of alienation and forces him to adapt, to make some adjustments. That resignation can be observed in the young men's looks, in their actions, and in their tendency to disparage white people. . . . Life has taught the young black man that he can do certain things but cannot go beyond his limited situation; dreams are simply never fulfilled." It has taught him, in short, that he is trapped on a road to nowhere, and that perhaps the only honorable thing to do is to die with dignity.

That misbegotten quest for honor too often leads to tragedy—not only for the young men abandoned by society, but for anyone who chances to get in their way. To their credit, many blacks (including some who are custodians of the criminal justice system) are searching for ways to get beyond that lose-lose situation. Betty DeRamus introduces us to several such exceptional individuals, including the memorable Willie Lipscomb, a Detroit judge who prefers turning people around to locking them up, and who has made it his mission to persuade young people to give up their guns.

As DeRamus explains, "Lipscomb began the Handgun Intervention Program . . . after nineteen-year-old, college-bound Kowan Comer, a boy he loved like a son, was shot to death at a party. Starting HIP in 1993 was Lipscomb's response to the shock of losing Comer. Under the program, bail-bond-seeking defendants who are charged with carrying concealed weapons—people who usually get probation if convicted—attend HIP's three-hour Saturday-morning class. Defendants as young as ten and as old as sixty-five have shown up for sessions, but most are in their late teens and early twenties. Usually, they come only once, but sometimes a judge orders them to return. Lipscomb made one young man who was arrested for carrying an AK47 attend thirty sessions of HIP." And the results, reveals DeRamus, have been astounding. Virtually none of the defendants who attend the program return with new charges within six months. Lipscomb's experience in losing a friend was not the only force propelling him to seek out an alternative way of life for gun-obsessed young black males: "His concern started in the late 1970s when he was a Wayne County prosecutor, specializing in murder cases. He was struck—no, shattered—by the autopsy reports. 'I saw one little young nineteen year old after another, dead with one gunshot wound in the chest,' he recalled. 'All of the autopsy protocols were the same—healthy, well-nourished young black males. . . . I started to see how guns would devastate young black men.'"

Young black men, of course, are not the only victims of pointless violence. Nor are black prosecutors the only ones conflicted over the prospect of sending felonious black men to prison. As Anita Hill makes clear, black women—particularly those who have been brutalized by the men they love—sometimes find themselves torn between the mandates of the law and loyalty to an abusive man. Hill recounts the story of Felicia and Warren Moon: a former cheerleader and a professional football player who, like Nicole and O. J. Simpson, briefly came to be seen in some circles as the public face of domestic violence. The Moon case came to light because a horrified child called 911 to exclaim, "My daddy is going to hit my mommy." Police ultimately found a bruised Felicia Moon, who allowed them to photograph the injuries she had suffered at her husband's hands and who told of fleeing the house in fear, but who refused to press charges. When prosecutors insisted on taking the case to court anyway, she testified in such a way—effectively taking all the blame for the incident herself—as to make her husband's conviction impossible. The issue in Felicia Moon's mind apparently was not just that of loyalty to a spouse, but to a spouse who she evidently felt had been unfairly targeted for racial reasons. As Hill writes: "Felicia Moon did what many women do: she stood by her man. But more than devotion to Warren Moon may have led to her choice. For Felicia Moon, a whole host of factors, some that she mentioned and others that were drawn from the circumstances, might have led her to resist filing charges and testifying. Money, fame, gender, and race all entered into the equation. Few of us dared to say what we instinctively knew was the truth: Felicia Moon could easily have been driven by a desire to save the reputation of a well-known Black man not only for himself but for the entire African American community. She ultimately decided that the loss of her reputation would be less damaging to her standing in the community than would be her disloyalty to a Black male hero."

To understand community loyalty to black men who are not good people (to men who beat their wives or prey on vulnerable people in their own communities) it is necessary to look beyond the individual miscreant and to the larger issue of racial persecution. One does not have to be an extremist to agree with Paul Butler's observation that a third of black men cannot be dangerous or evil, that there is something fatally wrong in a system (or with a society) that puts so many black people in jail. The very fact that so many black men are being consumed by the prison industry is enough to cause many people to rally, almost reflexively, around virtually anyone denounced by white authority. By the same token, distrust of black law enforcers is not an irrational sentiment lacking an antecedent. As Roger Wilkins points out: "The history of using blacks against other blacks has deep roots in slavery. There were brutal black overseers. There were also black informers. Plans for slave insurrections and escapes were often betrayed by other slaves seeking the masters' favor. In later generations, some blacks in law enforcement played out those roles, having concluded that they were accountable only to white power. Blacks working in the order-keeping system today carry the burden of that history."

Clearly, however, we are no longer in the age of slavery—or even Jim Crow. So to what extent is the history of a blatantly racist age relevant to black behavior today? Stanley Crouch argues that its relevancy has obvious limits. Similarly, suggests Crouch, arguments about the disproportionate impact of the justice system on blacks may be somewhat overblown: "Even if we accept the idea that the justice system unfairly tilts punishment toward lower-class black defendants and that the penal system imprisons a disproportionate number of convicted black men, we have to wonder what this idea actually means when we balance it against the equally disproportionate numbers of murders, rapes, robberies, and assaults that black people suffer at the hands of other black people who reside in the same communities. The yearly body counts extend far beyond what they were in even the most brutal periods of redneck Southern rule and Northern race riots." At some point, argues Crouch, rationalizations rooted in suppositions about consequences of a history of oppression must give way to some notion of free will, to some sense of individual responsibility. Moreover, the very fact of Simpson's acquittal is clear evidence of how much things have changed. As Wade Henderson points out, "Just two generations ago, a black man who was accused of Simpson's crime would have been lucky to survive the trial, much less be acquitted by a 'jury of his peers' for killing a white woman, at least in the South."

Is Clarence Page therefore right to suggest that it may be time for a reassessment? Can blacks forever think of ourselves as outsiders in our own country? Crouch believes the only sensible answer to the latter question is no. There is a certain lunacy, he contends, in the notion that we are defined solely by race, that our aspirations, our behavior, or our place in society should be dictated by race. At the center of the Simpson controversy, writes Crouch, "is the question of whether or not one's actions can yet be assessed on individual terms. . . . Was it possible for O. J. Simpson to be an individual first and a Negro either second or only incidentally? Was it possible for a predominantly black jury to be a gathering of individual experiences and perspectives instead of largely a mass of Pavlovian darkies ready to drool in unison at the opportunity to vent revenge on a legal system demonstrably mottled by racism?"

Darden clearly believes that, in many quarters, the answer is no, that despite his best efforts, his individuality (as far as much of the public was concerned) was subsumed within a racial stereotype. Yet, as Crouch points out, Darden had his own somewhat stereotypical ideas about race. When Darden writes, for instance, about "responsibilities as a human being" being "as important as the responsibilities of being an African American," does he mean to imply that those responsibilities are somehow in conflict? And, if in fact they are, what does that say not just about the justice system but about the fate of blacks in this country? Indeed, the larger issue raised by Darden, as well as many of the writers in the collection, is, "What does it mean to be a black person in America today?" To what extent is America truly our country too? To what extent will we continue to be defined—by ourselves and by the larger society—by stereotypes of criminality and intellectual defeat? How long, to put it bluntly, will black people in America continue to be "niggers"? Such questions ultimately can only be answered by African Americans, but they must be answered within the context of a society that clings to its stereotypes and that remains uncertain of what to make of its darker citizens.

However they perceive Darden, though, all the contributors agree that the Darden Dilemma is only one element in a much larger set of problems having to do with race and justice in America, and that that larger set of problems must be addressed. In an era in which more and more young black men (and boys) are coming to view a stint in jail as an inevitable rite of passage, it is not alarmist to point out that something has gone horribly wrong in

America, and that as judges send more and more blacks to prison, they may also be destroying America's long-cherished dream of racial equality. At some point—and one hopes it is long before we have turned vast parts of our nation into penal colonies—Americans must face up to the fact that prison is a poor substitute for effective social policy. Without doubt, violent criminals belong off the streets, and many of them should spend their natural lives behind prison bars—or as far from human prey as the law and human ingenuity can keep them. Yet, as many of the authors of this collection suggest, street crime does not break out in a vacuum; it typically thrives in environments that are not only impoverished financially, but that lack strong social, educational, and family support networks and that offer no compelling reason to believe in a better future. Until we, as a society, become as eager to provide those things for young black men as we are to provide them with jail cells, future Christopher Dardens will continue to face a dilemma—as they wonder whether they were truly placed on this earth for the primary purpose of putting other blacks behind bars; and future black jurors will find themselves sorely tempted to weigh the option—even if they know it to be wrong—of freeing black defendants simply because of the color of their skin.

Brotherman:
Reflections of a Reformed Prosecutor
PAUL BUTLER

I. PROSECUTOR

I am ten years old and riding my bicycle in Chicago. With the abandon of youth, I have pedaled to a shopping mall in an all-white neighborhood. Soon a cop car pulls alongside me, and the white officer leisurely rolls down his window. "You," he says, "is that bike yours?" "Yes," I answer, "is that car yours?" I speed off then but the spirit of the day is gone.

When I get home, I tell my mother—my militant, Malcolm-loving, King-marching, Afrocentric (before there was a word for Afrocentric) mother—what happened. She whups my ass but good. Don't I know what happens to black boys who talk to the police that way?

Twenty years later, I am a prosecutor. I am very good. In my black city, I love to stand in front of the black jurors and point, like I learned in training, at the black defendant. I represent the United States of America, I boast, and I am going to present evidence that proves beyond a reasonable doubt that that guy over there is a big jerk. Then I proceed to kick a little butt myself.

It is easy. Half the defendants are stupid, and the other half think they know more about the law than I do. The stupid ones I cross-examine at breakneck speed, tripping them on their own lies until the jurors sit back in disgust, ready to convict.

For the jailhouse lawyers, my pace is more deliberate, a series of precise questions intended to feign a search for truth:

Good guy: Where were you the evening the police testified they saw you selling crack?

Bad guy: Over to my baby's mother's house.

Good guy: Well, what is your wife's name?

Bad guy: Her name LaShaunda, but she not my wife.

Good guy: Where does Miss LaShaunda reside?

Bad guy (glancing at his defense attorney): Round my way. I just know the house, not the address.

Good guy: What is her telephone number?

Bad guy: I don't have to give that out.

Judge: Answer the question.

Bad guy: I don't remember.

Jury: Guilty.

Gentle reader, can you hear the slightest hint of sarcasm in my voice when I say "wife"? Do you see my eyes roll? Every time the bad guy slurs his words and trips over the conjugation of a verb, my diction becomes more precise; it emphasizes the excellence of my speech. I know how, at the end of a good cross-examination, to button my jacket and glance at the jurors in a manner that affirms the difference between African Americans—they and I—and niggers, the genus of the criminal defendant.

I have the best conviction record in the misdemeanor section.

II. Persecutor

I share with Christopher Darden a contempt for many criminal defendants. They are assholes, a large percentage of them, and almost all are guilty. I never prosecuted one who wasn't guilty, no matter what the jury thought. The worst of them are big bullies who prey on the weak. Several of the defendants I saw in misdemeanor court reminded me of the guys from junior high who beat me up because I got good grades and had a mother who picked me up after school in a car. From simple assault, those dudes had graduated to stickups or car thefts or beating the hell out of women. It was a type I got a big personal charge out of sending to prison—call it Revenge of the Nerd.

Those cases represented only about half my load; the

other half were druggies: users, either pitiful or unlucky, and the capitalist sellers. I didn't really have a personal opinion about their morality, so I espoused the opinion of my client, the United States. I was, after all, a hired gun. At a sentencing hearing, the United States thought something like this:

Your honor, the government requests a period of incarceration. This is not the defendant's first appearance in this court. He has failed to heed the warnings that other judges have given, and now it is time for him to be punished. He will continue to sell cocaine as long as he is out on the street. A year in the penitentiary would protect the citizens from his drug dealing, and it would give the defendant a chance to think about whether he wants to continue his life of crime. The penitentiary is not a pleasant place, so I hope his answer after a year would be no. And at least for that year, our citizens wouldn't have to worry about his threat to our community.

I learned during court proceedings always to refer to the bad guy as the defendant and certainly never to call him Mister. Referring to him as the defendant dehumanized him, making him more susceptible to conviction and punishment. Yet, for the sake of decorum in the courtroom, *the defendant* was more respectful than *cretin*, *douche bag*, and *asshole*, the words prosecutors used among themselves.

Druggies were about the biggest cretins because at the president's direction, we were not waging a war on guns or rape or public corruption but, rather, on drugs.

So at a closing argument or sentencing, I was able to work up as much froth over a drug user as over a violent criminal. It was pure technique, an actor's trick when he has no personal wellspring of emotion from which he can draw.

When I joined the prosecutor's office, I promised myself that I never would use drugs again. This was not a difficult promise to make; my previous consumption had been rare and recreational.

The fact that I had to make the promise at all indicates that, morally speaking, I was more offended at the thought of being a hypocrite than of being a possessor of controlled substances. When I consumed drugs, I could not have cared less that I was breaking the law; my exclusive concern was not to get caught. So as a prosecutor I found myself enforcing laws I had not respected as a private citizen. I don't mean to make this sound like a problem because it wasn't. After a while, prosecuting people for drugs became rote, like the routine part of any job that is comfortable because it is familiar. The problem didn't occur to me until much later, after I had prosecuted hundreds of people for drug crimes.

III. PROBLEM

My great-grandmother, whose own grandparents were slaves, hated white people and lectured me on why, as a survival skill, I should hate them also. St. Ignatius College Prep, Yale College, and Harvard Law School bred any residual malevolence out of me, but left a healthy suspicion. Yet this distrust seldom reared itself in the prosecutor's office because, like any army at war, we enjoyed an esprit de corps that was all consuming. We were fighting the good fight for the citizens of our community, and if we were mostly white and the citizens were mostly black, so what? The Lord doesn't care what color His workers are. We did our jobs well. A report was released that said that on any given day more than 40 percent of the young black men in our city were in the criminal justice system—either in jail, awaiting trial, or on probation or parole. We didn't talk about that report, at least not in any official way. Officially, we had pleas to bargain, cases to try, prisons to fill, a city to save. Our job was to make the statistics, not to interpret them.

Eventually, I left the prosecutor's office, burned out by the criminal defendants, who never stopped coming, and frustrated by many of my colleagues: the black prosecutors who thought but did not speak and the white prosecutors who spoke but did not think. Why were we always so busy? Why did so many black people commit crimes? What were the consequences to the community of putting so many black people in prison? Could anyone imagine a world like ours only with the races of the actors reversed: a white city with almost half the young white men either locked up or on their way to being locked up? And by black prosecutors! Could anyone even imagine that?

I came to law through teaching, where it was my business to interpret and imagine. What needed to be understood was staggering: more black men in prison than white men, even though black men are only 12 percent of the male population. More young black men in prison than in college. One-third of young black men under criminal justice supervision. What does all that mean? I imagined it depended on the crime.

About 60 percent of the people who are incarcerated for violent crimes in the United States are African American. The fact that those black people are locked up is, I think, pretty neat. It is good news for the vast majority of other black people who are most likely to be their victims. And it is good news for the country; in a sick kind of way, it is evidence of progress because for most of its history, the United States has not been especially concerned about using the criminal law to protect African Americans. The law has been used more as an instrument with which white supremacists oppress black people. Which brings me back to the drug laws.

The government's own statistics show that black people represent about 13 percent of people who use drugs but almost 75 percent of people who are imprisoned for drug crimes. In other words, black people don't use drugs any more than do white people—a fact that surely will not surprise anyone who has ever been on a college campus. African Americans just go to prison for doing so more. The result is that almost half the black people who are locked up are there for drug crimes. When we wonder about why there are so many black people in the system, drugs account for about half the answer.

In my criminal-law class students learn that the criminal justice system is supposed to treat people who are dangerous or immoral. I am embarrassed to teach this part of class—the justifications of punishment—because my students, mostly white, know that American prisons are filled with people who are black like me. I feel as though I am indicting my race with my own words. Yet to the accusation of dangerousness I must concur, reluctantly, that many of us are guilty as charged. I agree with the Reverend Jesse Jackson, who says that when he walks in my city late at night and hears the voices of men behind him, he feels safer when he looks back and sees that they are white, not black.

As to the immoral among us, however, I have a different experience. American history gives the white majority a near monopoly on immorality and explains the disproportionate rate of violence by blacks: Black people are more violent because they are victims of poverty and racism, sort of a one-two punch. Simply put, in a country where money means everything, not having any or a meaningful legal way to earn any debilitates folks, some to the point of violence. Racism—or, more descriptively, white supremacy—makes those desperate ones more likely to vent their rage on other black people because they are proximate, thanks to segregation, and because black lives are not as valuable, if you succumb to the doctrine that white supremacy promotes. And you have succumbed, though perhaps not to the degree that black violent criminals have. White supremacy is, after all, the dominant message of the culture, and black people are its most pitiful victims. I have heard, for example, that African Americans are the only ethnic group in the world whose image of God does not resemble themselves.

Meanwhile, back to the prosecutor's office: In the early evening, most of us escaped a long day of putting Negroes in prison and commuted to nice homes, as far away from black crime as one can get in a big city—which is to say, not far. Still our neighborhoods were flush with the accoutrements of the American middle class—lawns and Volvos and Starbucks—and shiny, happy people, mostly white. We lived in places that were different from the crime scenes we described to juries, venues with accoutrements of a different sort—liquor stores and lottery tickets and worn churches—and sullen people, mostly black, who should have witnessed the defendant's crime but might testify that they didn't see a damn thing.

If I was a thoughtful person, I might have explored the meaning of the white of our neighborhoods and the black of the criminal court. I might have wondered if the white people had money because they were smart and hardworking (the reason I thought I had money) and if those qualities also explained their absence from the criminal court, at least in the role of defendants.

If I was a thoughtful person, I might have asked, Why weren't the neighborhoods of most of the black people nearly as nice? Why didn't the black people have money? Was it their fault? And why was the criminal court so overwhelmingly black? Was it the same fault? I should have concluded that racism and poverty bore no relation to crime. If it did, wasn't I prosecuting people mainly because they were poor and black?

But these are questions I would have asked only if, when I was a prosecutor, I had been thoughtful. And I was not. It was a time when I could not afford thoughtfulness because as a black man it would have been too expensive.

IV. BLACK MAN

When a black man stops being a prosecutor, he should feel a little pensive. At the minimum, the way he has chosen to use his legal gifts ought to provoke thought. Not regret, necessarily, but serious introspection. I am assuming, of course, that he has done the regular work of the prosecutor, which is to put black men in prison.

What a black man should not do, when he stops being a prosecutor, is "dis" African American jurors. The Darden Dilemma is something that Christopher Darden made up to sell books and explain why he lost a relatively easy case. There are special problems that black prosecutors face, but black jurors are not among them. For me, they were the best aspect of my work.

When I rose from the government's bench and said, "My name is Paul Butler, and I represent the United States of America," the pride in the courtroom was almost palpable.

One real dilemma of black prosecutors is the danger of being a token, of allowing oneself to be paraded in front of black jurors but having white prosecutors call all the shots. Darden wrote that after his infamous mistake of asking Simpson to try on the bloody glove, he was shut out of major decisions involving the prosecution's trial strategy. Chris—my brother—I, like many other African American professionals, have been there and done that. In such situations, I have learned to inform my white colleagues that my black skin comes with a brain and that they don't get one without the other.

Tokenism is especially sinister in the context of prosecution because the prosecutor's race is being used to send a message to the jury that everything on the government's side is copacetic. Maybe this message is OK if the black prosecutor is serving this function; after all, the most persuasive argument in favor of black prosecutors is that their presence will make the prosecutor's office less racist. But if the prosecutor only makes an appearance at show time and is otherwise clueless, which Darden admits he was for a time, black people would be better off without him. Darden's malfeasance reminds me of Toni Morrison's dire accusation to a brother in a similar situation: You have taken your birthright and sold it for a mess of pottage.

The most difficult issue facing African American prosecutors is deciding what it means to be an integral part of a system that puts so many black people in prison. When a black man stops being a prosecutor, he ought to be especially thoughtful about his role in perpetrating American criminal "just-us."

When I left the prosecutor's office, I felt like a priest who leaves the church. Officially, those who leave the priesthood remain priests, yet they are considered to have abandoned their spiritual homes. I abandoned mine because God got a little confusing, at least in His incarnation as Truth and Justice.

What is justice for black victims of racism and poverty? I am convinced that punishment is not fair for predictable reactions to desperate circumstances. Prison is not the answer for every black lawbreaker, no matter what white legislatures say. I wrote an academic article in which I suggested that black jurors ought to be thoughtful about who they send to prison. Murderers, rapists, robbers: absolutely yes, for the safety of the community. But when black people are prosecuted for drug offenses and other victimless crimes, I recommended that jurors consider nullification—their legal power to ignore the written-down law in favor of a broader notion of justice.

All hell broke loose. One will never go broke overestimating the power of the black criminal to invoke America's wrath. Remember Willie Horton, the Scottsboro Men, and O. J. Remember Susan Smith and

Charles Stuart. Or just watch your local TV news this evening. The black outlaw is the boogeyman of the American Dream, its nightmare counterpoint. So to suggest that even nonviolent black criminals go free is a sure way to earn your fifteen minutes of infamy.

The article in the law review was featured on all the major network news programs. Mike Wallace interviewed me on *60 Minutes*. Montel Williams, Phil Donahue, Geraldo Rivera, and Rolanda Watts called. I made the front page of the *Wall Street Journal*. All for advocating the simple idea that when it comes to criminal justice, what is good enough for white people is good enough for African Americans. If whites are not routinely arrested, prosecuted, convicted, and sentenced to prison for certain conduct, blacks should not be either.

That apparently is a radical notion. I had hoped my article would engender some debate in the academic community. I had not expected death threats. But I also had not expected the proposal for jury nullification to receive such enthusiasm from people of all races. One of the most common questions I have been asked by progressive white people is, "May I nullify, too?" America locks up more of her citizens than any other supposedly free country in the world. If African Americans, by any means necessary, can effect the radical change that our criminal justice system needs, I predict that white people will be the first to thank them. It would not be the first time in our history that African

Americans saved white people's butts, morally speaking.

I found two reactions to the piece particularly interesting. One was the number of people who argued that the fact that so many African American people are under criminal justice supervision does not mean that the system is racist. I even heard this argument from some African Americans. What else but racism could be the meaning of the ugly statistics about the disproportionate number of black men in the system? However, with due respect for the power of white supremacy, it has not persuaded all black people that they are better off with one-third of their young men under governmental control.

Perhaps my reaction seems more emotional than rational, especially since I have conceded that as a group, African Americans might be more dangerous than whites. I think emotion is an appropriate mode of analysis for racial matters, especially if the alternative is "logic"; Malcolm X reminded us that "what is logical to the oppressor isn't logical to the oppressed." I come from a long line of black people who subscribe to an epistemology that black preachers call "knowing what you know." Knowing what you know refers to those beliefs, often emotional, that are at the core of one's being and that precede or subvert education and other formal ways of knowing. I know that I know that one-third of my sisters and brothers are not dangerous or evil and that any system of law that places them under its supervision is morally bankrupt and in need of immediate subversion. The difficulty is how, not why. As to the necessity, my mind is closed.

A closed mind, I know, is a terrible thing for a scholar to admit, so allow me a learned response to the critique as well. Outside the context of criminal justice, there is legal authority for the proposition that a racially disparate *effect* is prima facie evidence of racial discrimination or otherwise indicative of a practice or policy that should be changed. Even the conservative Supreme Court has endorsed this proposition in cases of employment discrimination. I would extend the same analysis to the criminal law; if, proportionally, it is punishing so many more blacks than whites, that should be enough to make the case that something is dreadfully wrong.

Unfortunately, because crime is so closely connected to race in the United States, many people can't see this argument as "logical." I think, however, that President Clinton, of all people, understands. At a speech the day of the Million Man March, he said that white people ought to think about how they would feel if one out of three of their young men were in the criminal justice system. If that were America, instead of only Africa-America, I'll bet people would blame the system as much as the young men. I think many of them would adopt radical positions, like mine, because then they would understand that the system requires radical change. I just wish that President Clinton had the guts to back his understanding with progressive solutions, although politically I don't much blame him. Remember, once again, Willie Horton.

Remembering the meaning of Willie Horton and all his black brothers means that it will be impossible for African Americans to achieve justice through traditional politics, including exercising their hard-gained franchise. Perhaps "impossible" is too strong; it is better to say that it will take too long, and African Americans can't afford to wait, considering the emergency nature of the crisis. It will take too long because the only way African Americans win in our winner-take-all democracy is to persuade white people to vote with them. For matters of racial justice, that is really tough. If it took the white majority more than two hundred years to understand that slavery was wrong, and approximately one hundred years to realize that segregation was wrong (and still many don't understand), how long will it take them to perceive that American criminal justice is evil?

And in the meantime, what should African Americans do? When one's house is on fire, should one wait for the people who set the fire to put it out? The critique of my proposal that most surprised me, because it came from some African Americans, is that black people should not nullify because that would contradict the rule of law. Now I am not sure that this is true of jury nullification; actually it is a part of the law. But, for the sake of argument, so what if emancipating a black person who does not belong in prison contradicts the law? Isn't that all the more reason for African Americans to embrace it? I expected to hear defenses of the rule of law from white folks. The law is made by and for them—at least the privileged ones—and so their defense of it makes sense. But when I heard some black people embracing this mythology about law I wondered if they keep up with the news. If they have read any of the recent "race" opinions of the Supreme Court. Apparently not. If so, surely they would discover "legal realism," the scholarly term for the concept that my grandmother described by saying that "judges do what they want to do." They don't decide justice so much as make it up as they go along.

Imagine, for example, that the issue before a court is whether it is appropriate, in a school district with a history of discrimination, to lay off a more senior white schoolteacher in order to allow a black teacher to keep her job? The "law" says look to the Constitution but you and I know that the answer is not found there. If you woke up one of the framers of the Constitution in the middle of the night and asked him, he would say something like, "Wait a minute! Niggers teaching school??! How did they escape from my plantation?" Legal realism posits that the modern-day judge first would decide the result of the case, based on her political beliefs, and then write an opinion pretending like the answer came from the Constitution.

I guess I just assumed that black people, congnizant of their history, were all legal realists. The faith of some

African Americans in the virtue of following the law at all costs is evidence of a patriotism that would be charming if it were not so pathetic. So many African American lives hang, like strange fruit, on the necessity of black self-help. Not to engage in the self-help simply because you think it undermines the law means that you love the law more than you love your people. You have more in common with the black criminal than you probably realize. White supremacy has led both of you to cheapen your own worth.

The good news is that there are programs that stop crime more effectively and at less cost than prison. The bad news is that most people, particularly lawmakers, seem not to care. An empirical study by the Rand Corporation found that the best way to prevent crime is to provide financial and health services to poor children and their families. Per dollar spent, such intervention prevented more crime than sending offenders to prison. It makes sense, doesn't it? If people commit certain kinds of crimes because they are poor and hopeless, give them money and hope. That might sound more naive than it is, but as a society we certainly lavish money on offenders right now. California, for example, spends more dollars locking up its citizens than it does educating them. So the financial resources exist—the only question is whether we will use that money to help poor black people or to put them in boxes.

As long as we choose the boxes, I will advocate black self-help by any means necessary. Even Clarence

Thomas has acknowledged that when he looked out of his office window and saw young black men in chains marching into criminal court he thought, "There but for the grace of God go I." The determination of who goes into criminal court in chains should not be so fortuitous. It should not depend so much on race and class. It will depend, however, upon such irrelevant facts until wealth is distributed in this country on a nonracial basis, until health care is available to all, and until white supremacy is crushed. I doubt that day will come anytime soon. Meanwhile back at the prosecutor's office, another black man takes my place on the drug squad, locking up his brothers. I pray him wisdom and courage and another job.

Paul Butler is an associate professor at George Washington University Law School who specializes in criminal law and racial issues. Prior to his teaching career, he was a trial attorney at the U.S. Department of Justice, investigating and prosecuting public corruption cases. He has also served as a special assistant U.S. attorney, prosecuting drug and gun cases. His scholarship has been the subject of a Mike Wallace profile on 60 Minutes. He has appeared as an expert on public policy issues on the Today show, PBS's McLaughlin One on One, National Public Radio, and CBS, NBC, ABC, and Fox nightly news broadcasts.

Willie Lipscomb's Crusade
Betty DeRamus

I'd like all the niggers in the room to stand," deputy sheriff John Jones tells the defendants, all but three of them African American. Nobody stands. Nobody shouts, "I object." Nobody groans or even grins. They're all trying to figure out where this lawman plans to lead them. Around the block for a bag of cheap, greasy belly laughs? Back to Africa for a taste of Kunta Kinte's slave ship pain?

Or is this just some wired-up, word-happy, wiseguy-Christopher Darden with an earring and a summer suit—acting like they're the ones accused of knifing Nicole?

"Come on," says Jones, "I know somebody was a nigger last night or before you came in here. The very word [*nigger*] means ignorance. It was made up five hundred years ago when they brought blacks over here to be slaves. They made up that word to keep people down in bondage. Five hundred years later we're still using it. . . . You never heard no white people say, 'Hey, what's happening, honkey.' You never heard a Hispanic say, 'Hey, what's happening, wetback.' We never heard Chinese say, 'Hey, what's happening, Chink.' You ain't no nigger."

The courtroom looks like some bare-bones, bargain-basement church—plain wooden pews in back, people with power up front, and a furled flag in one corner representing dusty history and hopes. But Jones knows that no shouts of "Amen, brother" will sweep this congregation and make its members swoon and seep sweat—not even when he announces he has the telephone number of a professor who can get them college grants. This mostly young, mostly black, mostly male group didn't come to this courtroom in Detroit's Thirty-sixth District Court to see saints or stumble upon salvation. They came here with their "Newport Pleasure" T-shirts; thick-soled sneakers; and dazed, done-it-all eyes because a court magistrate sent them. They came because the black court officials, whom some of them might consider sellouts or Uncle Toms, don't want to see them in prison cells and coffins.

But there is no Darden Dilemma in this place, no conflict between sentencing black defendants to probation or jail and remaining a real "brother." This is a courtroom in which tattered young lives can still be tacked together. In this made-to-order church, the gospel truth comes from piles of homicide statistics, photographs of dead civil rights leaders, and a slide show of murder victims with mangled kneecaps and missing heads. The slide show packs so much power that even some gunwise defendants look away. It includes pictures of what's left of a drug dealer's body after it's been stashed in the trunk of a car for two weeks. Pictures of a seven- or eight-year-old boy caught in the crossfire of somebody else's anger and mowed down with a .357 magnum. Pictures of a man shot twelve or thirteen times with an Uzi, his head torn off, his body pockmarked with wounds. Pictures of people shot with small-caliber weapons—.22s and .25s—the bullets ricocheting inside their bodies and ripping up organs. With one or two exceptions, the victims were aged fifteen to twenty-four, just like these defendants. And with one or two exceptions, all were armed when they died.

The high priest here is Judge Willie Lipscomb. As a boy, Lipscomb longed to drive a big beast of a Greyhound bus, telling passengers, white and black, when to leap on and off. After a stint as an air force medic, he enrolled in the premed program of an open-admissions college. Later, he encountered some legendary local lawyers, and his dream grew wings and took off, landing in the lap of the law. Lipscomb, who was only a D student at Detroit's old Eastern High school, wound up with a juris doctorate from the University of Notre Dame. When he talks to youths, he points out his success with pride. "I think those of us who have skills, we need to brag a little bit more," he says. "[Young people] are waiting for us to recruit them."

Lipscomb began the Handgun Intervention Program (HIP) after nineteen-year-old, college-bound Kowan Comer, a boy he loved like a son, was shot to death at a party. Starting HIP in 1993 was Lipscomb's response to the shock of losing Comer. Under the program, bail-bond-seeking defendants who are charged with carrying concealed weapons—people who usually get probation if convicted—attend HIP's three-hour Saturday-morning class.

Defendants as young as ten and as old as sixty-five have shown up for sessions, but most are in their late teens and early twenties. Usually, they come only once, but sometimes a judge orders them to return. Lipscomb made one young man who was arrested for carrying an AK47 attend thirty sessions of HIP. "In this court," he said, "all you do is deal with misdemeanors [carrying sentences of] up to ninety days. We're involved in prevention. We're trying to avoid them getting caught up in serious felonies."

Lipscomb actually began worrying about the survival of young black men long before his teenage friend's murder. His concern started in the late 1970s when he was a Wayne County prosecutor, specializing in murder cases. He was struck—no, shattered—by the autopsy reports. "I saw one little young nineteen year old after another, dead with one gunshot wound in the chest," he recalled. "All of the autopsy protocols were the same—healthy, well-nourished young black males. . . . I started to see how guns would devastate young black men."

The judge's message that nobody's safe when everybody carries guns doesn't always hit home with young defendants right away, not even when the judge reveals that he quit carrying a gun himself. The judge, after all, is in his fifties, a man who comes to work in gray suits, a guy who represents something they call "the system." So sometimes the defendants shrug off the judge's predictions until they look up and see his words taking bloody shape in their lives. A girl who ignored warnings to be careful where she partied wound up one night in an after-hours joint surrounded by gunmen with roaring AK47s. She has since sent Lipscomb a letter of support. After the fatal shootings of both his best friend and the mother of his two children, a young man who claimed the program hadn't touched him also became a HIP promoter.

"We tell them if they don't do something about [handgun violence], it's going to hit somebody else, in your family, in your neighborhood," Lipscomb stated. "One of the participants said he went out and got his little cousins who were carrying guns in his little group and talked to them and got them to stop carrying guns. We're trying to create . . . community leaders who will go out into their neighborhoods. We're trying to plant a seed in them."

The HIP program is being duplicated in Flint, Michigan, and studied by the Washington-based Urban Institute; yet no one program can rescue all the young black men and, increasingly, women who are crowding the nation's courts, jails, and morgues. According to a 1990 study published in the *New England Journal of Medicine*, young men in Harlem are less likely to live to age forty than their counterparts in Bangladesh. And young black men who survive the streets all too often end up like Rick, a thirty-four-year-old former drug dealer who spent eight years in prison wondering each day whether he'd get a blade in his belly. Tougher drug laws that allow the same federal mandatory minimum sentence for every participant in a drug ring, regardless of how minor his role, will create more and more Ricks. Some observers, in fact, believe that the high prosecution and arrest rates for minorities prove that the War on Drugs is mostly a war on young, highly visible, and replaceable black street dealers.

"No one is suggesting that the street dealer is innocent," noted U.S. Representative John Conyers, Jr. (D-Detroit). "He is not. But neither is he the one flying planes to Colombia bringing back million-dollar cargoes."

Conyers has been leading the national fight to eliminate the 100–1 disparity between federal sentences for using and possessing crack cocaine and for using and possessing the powdered cocaine from which crack is made. Since high-level dealers and drug wholesalers are more likely to handle powdered cocaine, it makes no sense, critics say, to give them far lighter sentences than crack peddlers.

Jeffrey Edison, a criminal defense attorney in Detroit for twenty years, believes that the incarceration of black men "serves a purpose of destroying the African community by removing African men and isolating them during the most productive years of their lives. It's no [accident] that one out of four African men between 15 and 29 [has] been affected by the criminal justice system or incarcerated."

But Rick, the former drug dealer, believes "you have a choice in life," even if you live in a city where unskilled jobs have dried up, major industries have packed up and gone, and drug peddling and gun carrying have created a subculture of quick money and easy death. It's a culture in which children as young as six can buy bubble gum in black boxes that resemble drug dealers' beepers and clip them onto their belts. A culture in which fifteen-year-old crack dealers drive white Monte Carlos and wear $700 leather jackets. A culture in which young men proudly spray-paint "twenty-five and still alive" on the walls of schools and offices they will never legitimately step inside. A culture in which too many young people live for the moment, the hour, the too-short and often dangerous days.

Detroit hasn't been the "murder capital" of the United States for years. It lost that title long ago as one beleaguered city after another found itself bandaging wounds and sweeping up bullets. But it is a city in which a young woman named Deletha Word jumped into the Detroit River and drowned to escape a beating from a burly young man whose car she'd banged up. It's also a city in which at least two men plunged into the river that night, battling surging water and rising despair in an unsuccessful attempt to save Word's life. It's a city of skinny houses squeezed onto tiny lots like fat men in tight tubs. It's also a city of riverfront apartments with their own gyms and grocery stores. It's a city in which thousands of volunteers tow away tires, scoop up neighborhood trash, and board up open buildings. And it's a city of vacant lots that resemble virgin forests, the wildflowers tall enough to look you in the eye and laugh. It's a town of sunshine and shadows, of deserted side streets, and of slam-bang plans for new side-by-side football and baseball stadiums downtown. It's a place in which the caring and the cold often sit side by side, fighting for the city's soul.

In Detroit, some black educators and parents cope with the so-called Darden Dilemma by struggling, like Judge Lipscomb, to portray carrying and using guns as senseless and even stupid. All the same, some black youngsters grow up believing there's something wrong, something antiblack, about speaking standard English and chasing white-collar-and-tie success.

A substitute teacher came face to face with the problem in a school lunchroom. The five words he heard that day still haunt him. "Quit trying to eat white," one student yelled to another. Everybody at the table began chanting the words. The youngster under attack had made the mistake of cutting up his chicken with a knife instead of eating it with his hands. "I know it sounds petty," the teacher admitted in one of my columns (*Detroit News*, November 21, 1993), "but it just hit me like a ton of bricks. I suddenly realized that this was a major problem with many of our young people.

"They're afraid that if they prefer reading books to slam-dunking basketballs somebody is going to say they're acting white. They're worried that if they don't talk like the people in music videos they're going to be accused of talking white. This is a terrible thing because it implies that you have to fail in life or else conform to a certain image to be truly black. That makes me mad. Since when does being black have to mean only negative things?"

That teacher is not the only Detroiter who is tormented by such questions. Consider what these people are doing:

- A man who claims he was imprisoned for eleven years for a murder he didn't commit confronts dope dealers on their own turf, works for a youth center, and is sheltering a sixteen-year-old boy who is in danger of being swallowed up by streets with sharp teeth. He has had to deal with death threats from dealers and assassination plots.

- A man whose crack-addicted mother is serving a life sentence for murdering her husband leads marches on crack houses, knocking on dealers' doors and surrounding dope houses with candle-carrying, slogan-chanting marchers. In many cases, he's marching in the same neighborhoods where his boyhood friends have either surrendered to drugs or died.

- An auto executive, fearful that his children might grow up living and dying for leather coats and gold chains, refused to let his youngsters watch television or have telephones throughout their teenage years. Though the children gagged on their father's bitter medicine, it cured them of the disease of falling behind and then failing.

- A mother whose only son was found with a bullet hole in his forehead has begun a prison ministry for male and female inmates whom she lectures every week. In her battle to convince young people that they don't have to follow any street code or crowd, she is fighting everything from war games and war toys to forty-ounce servings of malt liquor.

Meanwhile, some blacks who are part of the criminal justice system agree that they have a special responsibility to do something to halt, or at least slow, the flood of young blacks jamming America's jails.

Danton Wilson, a Wayne County prosecutor, is forced to consider both sides of the criminal justice crisis—the need for law and order and the need for a humane system. When he sees all the African American defendants passing through the courts, he senses that there must be a better approach than just herding people into the system and dropping them into a hole. At the same time, he thinks it's important for people like him to be a part of the system.

"If you don't have a prosecutor's office and you don't have people willing to prosecute people who do things in our community, I think lawlessness would really be further out of control," he said. "I believe my presence and the presence of other African American prosecutors serves sometimes to put the brakes on cases that perhaps need to be massaged a little bit more, looked at a little bit closer." He lives with the tensions inherent in his job by making sure he always treats defendants and their families with respect.

Still, he has mixed feelings about winning some cases. "One of my fellow prosecutors put it really well the other day," Wilson said. "There are no real winners. By the time we get finished, the [victims] clearly [haven't] won because often they've lost a loved one or lost the kind of sense of security that comes from maybe not being victimized by a serious crime. And the person who is going to be incarcerated is clearly not going to be a winner. His family members, too, are in a sense victims because they're seeing a loved one lost."

Howard King, certainly, has no desire to see the walls, hear the screams, or smell the rage walled up inside any of Michigan's prisons. When he was twenty, he was imprisoned for second-degree murder, a crime he insists he didn't commit. Furthermore, he says, it was his dark dignity and size, his refusal to be branded a nigger, that led to his eleven-year stay in the State Prison of Southern Michigan.

It all started, he noted, back in 1964, when he was fourteen years old. He was on the streets one day, play-ing football. He was just a kid, but he already stood six feet tall, so he was playing ball with men. The police stopped and asked the group, "What are you niggers doing playing football in the street?" None of the adults responded, but King spoke up, explaining that there was glass on the playground and adding, "I'm not a nigger." After that, he said, he was struck with a nightstick, hauled off to a precinct in handcuffs, and led between two lines of police officers who kicked him in the groin and beat him in the head. He was freed, but according to King, the incident triggered years of police harassment. This was at a time when Detroit's police force was still predominantly white, living in white enclaves, and acting like "a foreign army of occupation," according to Coleman Young, the for-mer mayor of Detroit.

King wishes he had had someone to talk to during his teenage years, some kind of therapist, someone to tell him that not all white police officers are bad, just as not all blacks are criminals. He insists that his harassment led to the charge of second-degree murder trumped up by police officers. His first trial for the murder of a security guard ended in a hung jury, in part because a witness testified that the police had given her ounces of heroin to testify against King. In the second trial, a witness described the murderer as a light-skinned black man with a large Afro. King, who is dark skinned and has short hair, believes that an attorney like Johnnie Cochran could have won his freedom. However, unlike O. J. Simpson, King was not famous, had no fortune, and was assigned only a court-appointed attorney. "If I had O. J.'s money, it would have been a different outcome," he said. "By me being beat up by men in uniform when young, the prosecutor tried to make it [seem that] I had a thing against people in uniform."

In his first years in prison, King fantasized about getting revenge, but eventually those feelings faded. He made up his mind that once he was free, he'd counsel youths. But first he had to pass the hurdle of rejecting the dope man.

"The first day I come home, . . . the first person I see was this dope dealer who come to my house driving a Cadillac and his girlfriend was behind him driving a Mercedes Benz," he remembers. "He get out the Cadillac, and he come and hug me. Before I went up, he wasn't a drug dealer. He was thinking he was gonna recruit me with this car. He gave me the keys to his Cadillac. He says that's yours, and I throwed the keys back. When I looked back over my right shoulder, he was killing me with his eyes. But I'm not for sale."

These days, King works with youths at a community center and in his neighborhood, where the dope dealers send him death threats and once persuaded a woman to try to poison him. He shares his house with the sixteen-year-old half brother of his daughter, a young man who is not related to him but needed a haven from the streets. "I'm gonna do all I can to help these youths," King asserted.

For citizens like community activist Malik Shabazz, the answer to America's criminal justice crisis also is on the streets. Shabazz woke up one morning and realized that time was running out, moving faster than the men who collect drug debts with long guns under their trench coats. Already, his mother had crashed, condemned to life in prison for arranging the murder of her fourth husband—a murder-for-insurance scheme concocted while she was smoking crack. Most of Shabazz's boyhood buddies had climbed aboard the dope train, too. They patrolled the streets, peddling packets of crack and running foot races with bullets. They stumbled in and out of crack houses, chasing that five-minute high while the voices in their heads mocked them or yelled threats. The day his mother's trial started, Shabazz knew his time was up.

Shabazz's mother is Andrea Wilson Gumar. As the stepdaughter of a state senator, she had been raised for a life of wide living rooms and deep swimming pools and later became a registered nurse and a policeman's wife. But she had led a secret life as "Belinda," smoking $250 worth of crack a day and hanging out with people like Mack Gumar, an alleged dope dealer and pimp. After the murder of her fourth husband, Detroit police-man Jimmie Wilson, Andrea married Mack Gumar, but it was no love match. During the couple's trial, Mack testified that he had been attracted to Andrea's 1981 Cadillac and motorboat. At any rate, the two were con-victed of setting up Wilson's murder, presumably for his $100,000 life insurance policy. It tore Malik Shabazz's family to pieces. It rippled through all their lives, spreading shock and pain, just like the deaths of most of Shabazz's boyhood friends. In 1994, Shabazz, a minis-ter in a small, African-centered spiritual church, began knocking on the doors of crack dealers and marching on their businesses—the fear of death on one shoulder and the fear of life as it was on the other.

Shabazz was in his early thirties then, a cream-col-ored black man who stands six feet, five inches, the nat-ural center of any crowd. When he first began march-ing, he was joined by two or three other men, five or six children, and maybe fifteen women. The first time, they staged an all-day rally on an east-side street with four crack houses. The next target was a party store that sold crack and rotten sandwiches; it has since closed. After the Million Man March in 1995, more men began join-ing Shabazz. His band marched ten times in 1995, sometimes in blinding heat or in below-zero cold. In

July 1996, fifty marchers, thirty-five of them men, took their prayers and persistence to an abandoned bank that had been taken over by a crew of firebomb-tossing crack dealers. Nobody tried to stop them when they padlocked the place.

Shabazz has his detractors, including people who believe that he must be on drugs himself or taking pay-offs to end his boycotts against merchants who peddle bad meat. Others say he's wasting his time, chasing drug dealers from one spot to the next. Still, he's con-vinced that his crusade against crack has changed some minds, some hearts, and some communities near col-lapse.

"I don't want any other family to have to go through what mine had to go through," he said. "I want to do all I can to alleviate the pain and the misery and the suffer-ing. When someone's addicted to drugs, it's not just that person who's a victim. Everybody who loves them, who knows them, becomes a victim. For every person that's addicted to drugs, there's possibly fifty people who are directly affected by it. [Drug addiction] increases crime. It increases every kind of thing. What my mother did almost destroyed my family. It'll never be the same."

Talk and tears aren't enough for Akua Chenyere Yisrael, either. In July 1996, she carried her dead son's ashes to Ghana and sprinkled them on the waters of a flirty little stream rushing off to meet a churning river. In his twenty-five years of stumbling through life,

Chenyere's son, James Aaron Williams Jr., had never imagined such a swirl of white water and green mountains. In 1995, he died in a blast of gunfire in Lansing, Michigan, he and his girlfriend both shot in the center of their foreheads. At first glance, their deaths looked like two more drug-related slayings, two more eruptions of death in the dark. Williams's girlfriend, after all, was a known user of crack cocaine who might have had debts that only blood could pay off. However, Williams owned the murder weapon, and the police claimed it bore only his fingerprints.

Williams drank Colt 45 malt liquor, a drink whose very name conjures up images of smoking guns on the billboards cramming inner cities. Maybe he smoked a little weed sometimes, too, chasing the marijuana from his forty-ounce bag with forty ounces of malt liquor. Perhaps Williams was speeding down the highway to depression and crashed. Or perhaps someone forced his hand to grip a gun. Nobody knows for sure why this young man—locked up for a year as incorrigible after his parents' divorce—died with a bullet in his head.

All his mother knows is that she doesn't want other young men and women to suffer her son's fate because they followed a crowd or a craze. A physical therapist who works with mentally and physically developmentally disabled children, Chenyere is a woman whose thoughts and feelings quickly harden into plans. Weeks after her first exposure to Mortal Kombat video games, she wrote a manifesto against war games and toys and passed it on to sponsors of a congressional hearing on the subject. Nowadays, she leads a weekly support group for men and women at a prison in a Detroit suburb. She urges these young men and women to find their purpose, to uncover their buried gifts, to choose life.

"I first tell them why it is that I'm there," she said, "let them know that I believe in their divinity and that I don't believe anybody got on the planet without God's permission . . . and with that being said, I go on to tell them that the one thing I know about them without knowing anything about their history is that they're not on that divine mission."

Ted Dowl faced the Darden Dilemma when he risked losing his children's love so he could save them. Dowl still remembers the day he decided that the best way to keep his son and daughter from failing in school and life was to clear his house of all telephones, television sets, cigarettes, and liquor. His children were then eleven and twelve years old. His moment of decision came when he arrived at a football game and watched his daughter from a distance: She was all decked out in gold chains, designer boots, and blue jeans and wearing a look that said, "Hey, look at me." Dowl said: "I stood back and said, 'Is this what I'm creating?'"

He cleaned house, forcing his kids to read more and pour more time and energy into their homework and family activities. It was a tough step, alienating friends, family members, and, initially, his children. "They [his children] thought they would just die," he said. "My daddy talked about me, my mother talked about me, my mother-in-law talked about me. They said you can't do it. I said watch me."

According to Dowl, both youngsters turned themselves around after he eliminated all distractions and forced them to focus on learning. His son is now an entertainer in Chicago, and his daughter manages a communications company. Meanwhile, Dowl has become a member of the Nile Valley Study and Research Institute, a group of black Detroiters who travel extensively and study the contributions of blacks throughout world history, sharing this knowledge in middle schools, high schools, and colleges and occasionally in prisons.

"We have to take our minds back," said Dowl, superintendent of final assembly at the Dearborn Assembly Plant. "We were not [lifelong] slaves in Africa. You could be a slave today and a king or governor tomorrow. But the world today would have us think . . . we've a body and no mind. . . . We are faced with a crisis, and the way out of the crisis is to change the program. We have to change from [acquiring] material things to understanding who we are and regaining respect for our mothers and this temple of a body we're residing in."

Crime and punishment. Struggling parents and endangered children. Black crime and white reactions. . . . In the days when I wrote a column for the *Detroit News*, a major metropolitan daily with hundreds of thousands of readers, I wrote about all this from the safe distance of an air-conditioned office with security guards in the lobby. All that changed when a newspaper strike hit Detroit in July 1995, and I walked off my job. As I write this piece, the strike continues, a new Civil War, pitting friend against friend, new employees against old, strikers against the editors, who, in some cases, recruited or groomed them. Meanwhile, I have come home, once again writing for the black weekly newspaper where I began my career.

In part, I think I was searching for an old dream, the joy of no longer having to bear the burden of proving myself every day or dealing with readers who accused me of trying to spark a riot whenever I dipped my toes into the waters of controversy. On the one hand, many of my white readers seemed to think that talking about a problem, such as the disproportionate number of blacks in jail, was itself the problem—that frank talk sparked dissension, disorder, and even riots. My black readers, on the other hand, seemed to believe it was far more dangerous to sit on problems than to expose them to the light of debate. The O. J. Simpson case did not create any new racial divide or chasm. It only highlighted the radically different perspectives that black and white Americans sometimes bring to issues like police brutality and harassment, racial history and pain. The case snatched off the polite coverings, the colorless chitchat, that often muffle interracial communication. For a while at least, frank talk became fashionable, but I knew it wouldn't last.

To keep my sanity, I eventually developed a formula, 85 percent of the time writing "feel-good" stuff about people overcoming odds or battling social problems. Then just when everybody had relaxed and decided I was no threat to the public peace, I would write a piece saying that thirty years ago some poor, bewildered black man would have been dragged out of his bed and hanged on the strength of Susan Smith's spurious claim that a black man had killed her children. Of course, not all (or even a majority of) my white readers were the kind of people who'd send me unsigned postcards saying that I'd never have gotten my job without affirmative action. The silent majority were well-meaning, thoughtful, and even loving people. Sometimes, however, even they wanted more from me than I could safely give. On one occasion, I had to escort the wife of a former boss to a children's center I'd written about so she could donate some toys. It was a rough area, and her husband didn't think she should go alone. If we'd been attacked, I don't know how he thought that I—a medium-sized, middle-aged woman with no weapons other than running shoes—could have defended her. Did he see my blackness as some sort of shield, a coat of protective paint tough enough to deflect bullets?

These days, I no longer have to ponder such questions or spend every waking moment trying to prove that I deserve my salary. But my safety net is gone, too, my ivory-tower life and my separation from the sometimes-desperate people I profile.

The crisis that puts so many blacks behind bars or in untimely graves is more than statistics or trends or quotes from experts. It is more than a splashy once-in-a-lifetime case like the Simpson saga. It is Rick, and James Aaron Williams, and thousands of others like them. It is Debrah.

The year her laughter stopped and her crying started, Debrah was twenty-nine. She was willing to sample, smoke, or sell whatever the men in her life wanted. Wayward as streets with bullet holes in stop signs and shoe prints on smashed doors. Wild. She sold crack from the front porch of a house on the east side of Detroit, peddling it to packs of junkies who stood around like puppies praying for pizza. With a dope supply house right across the street, Debrah could skip over in seconds and scoop up another $500 sack of crack.

She came from a good home, not quite the Cosby family but close enough: one sister, one brother, a mother who was a nurse, and a father who worked at the Fisher Body plant. Nobody in her house smoked, snorted, or shot up drugs, but her father occasionally drank. The whole family attended church on Sundays, and when she was in junior high school, Debrah hurried straight home from school and burrowed into her homework. Then, the father who'd kept the family under control, who spelled out its rules, died.

Debrah quickly learned that she could get away with things without being punished. Her family no longer had a stern prosecutor, someone who would say "no." She began taking her clothes to school in a gym bag and going to friends' homes after school to smoke weed and meet her boyfriends. Men always liked her upturned eyes and full, sweeping lips. She had her first son in the twelfth grade, a month before graduation. By age eighteen or nineteen, she had two kids. And at nineteen going on twenty, she was on her own. The boyfriend who introduced her to crack wound up getting shot in the head seven times. Another boyfriend left her after he returned home from prison and discovered that she'd slept with a dealer to get crack. Her current boyfriend is doing time for violation of probation: carrying a concealed weapon and breaking into a coin box.

In 1995, Debrah was arrested three times on drug charges and spent three months in jail. Only her pregnancy and a drug habit saved her from the sort of sentence America likes to slap on nonviolent offenders who drive Jeeps without licenses and hide crack pipes between their legs. After a year of probation in a community residential treatment program, she now has a shiny new desk drawer of dreams—to attend community college; become an executive secretary; regain the trust of her mother, whom she manipulated with lies for years; and regain custody, or at least the company, of her two older sons.

I used to believe that people like Debrah should all be rounded up and locked up some place far from the path of trouble, away from all their crack and confusion. I thought that if young people watched their street heroes fall, they'd become disillusioned with drugs and guns.

I was wrong.

Make no mistake. I still believe that people who break the law should suffer consequences and suffer them quickly—not after they've run up a rap sheet of fifteen or twenty offenses. There ought to be a whole string of alternatives, including enough drug-treatment centers to accommodate immediately those addicts who decide to quit. A few years ago, a thirteen-year-old boy was tried as an adult for armed robbery in Miami. What struck me the most about his case was that he had more than fifteen arrests by the time he wound up in court charged with robbing a man at gunpoint. Until then, his crimes and truancies had been blinked away, dismissed as boyish pranks. They shouldn't have been. There should have been some program that boy could have entered when he swiped his first candy bar at age six.

What I'm seeing in this country is something quite different. I see legislatures expanding the list of crimes for which juveniles can automatically be waived to adult courts. I see states removing the age barriers at which children can be incarcerated in adult jails and prisons. I see governors sending juvenile offenders to privately run youth prisons, creating industries that are hungry for more and more young bodies. I see officials riding into office on the promise that they will "lock 'em up forever."

The criminal justice system sometimes seems to be a game in which everybody plays a part and justice is expected to be the outcome. Sometimes justice prevails, but many times it doesn't. But the game of justice becomes too transparent when you listen to a 250-pound police officer swear that he succeeded in chasing and catching a lean, lightning-quick eighteen year old just as he was dropping a bag of dope.

All too often what happens in criminal trials seems less a search for justice than a contest between opposing forces, a war for the soul of the jury. What results may represent justice, or it may not. A Detroit financial analyst who served on an all-black jury in 1992 remarked that other jurors were ready to convict the defendant because—unlike O. J. Simpson—this accused car thief swaggered into court in a wide-brimmed hat and white cashmere coat and talked as though he'd just strolled in from the streets. It didn't help matters that a policeman let it slip that the man had a drug case pending against him.

Or as attorney Jeffrey Edison put it: "By the time you get to trial, you have a witness who is testifying who may or may not be testifying truthfully. [Witnesses'] ability to express credible testimony depends on how well they articulate what it is they're saying and the manner in which they testify, their demeanor on the stand, their lawyers' demeanor, the manner in which they [the lawyers] ask questions. . . . The verdict may be one consistent with the reality, but often times it is not. The African male has been criminalized throughout the media. The [best] example of that was Willie Horton . . . in the presidential campaign . . . and then you have *Time* magazine's shading O. J. three or four shades darker [and therefore, more criminal] on the cover."

It is about 12:15 P.M. on a Saturday morning, and some fifty defendants, a dozen observers, and four young children crowd Judge Lipscomb's courtroom. Some of the defendants sit with their arms extended, creating a circle of protective space around them. Others keep their arms folded tightly in front of them, a layer of bone against all those bullets out there. They have been sitting like this for hours, listening to speakers, looking at slides, staring at statistics. They heard Judge Lipscomb tell them that there are 1.4 million people in America's prisons and that more and more are being sent every day.

The judge warned them that when they carry guns, they're playing "somebody else's game. When you play somebody else's game, you lose every time." Lipscomb compared carrying guns to playing three-card monte with a trickster who lets you win in the beginning and then snatches your money. He compared it to a bunch of big guys trying to play shake-and-bake basketball with lithe little guys who run all over them.

"Play your game," he said. "Ever had a coach tell you

that? Don't play the other team's game. An illusion has been created in your mind that you're winning, but actually you're losing very badly. This is about big money. That's what we're missing in this issue.

"Who's got some stock in Smith & Wesson? Raise your hands. Who's got some stock in Winchester? Who's got some stock in Remington? Nobody in here? You must have some stock in Midwest casket. Do you? [If not], then it looks like you playing somebody else's game to me."

He already told them about the Moors, the Africans who established an empire in Spain during the Middle Ages. He also told them that they are the descendants of kings and, therefore, are princes themselves. Yet as long as they think of themselves as "niggers," he said, that's all they'll ever be—not lawyers, not pilots, not businesspeople, and certainly not good parents. He even showed them photographs of people who had the courage to go to the South during the civil rights movement, risking their lives for the right to vote and the right to rest in the front of a hot bus.

Now, the preacher is winding up his sermon and looking for the payoff, some proof that his words have raised temperatures and touched souls. He asks two young defendants to step forward and read aloud a vow of nonviolence. The room is filled with the sound of defendants repeating the pledge: "Guns and violence will kill our people. I claim my heritage as a leader and disavow guns and violence." Then the judge asks all the defendants to sign copies of the vow and take the copies home with them, so they can frame them and tell their friends and families what the vow means.

"If it's in your heart to do it," he says, "stand up right now. Step out and be leaders out here in this community. You gonna get some respect when you make Detroit the Canada of this country."

After Judge Lipscomb issues his call, his plea for these young people to come up to the baptismal fountain and be reborn, I hold my breath. Will these young men and women ignore all the history and hope, passion and poetry, pumped into this room for three fast-moving hours? Will they keep sitting behind folded arms and locked hearts? Then suddenly, all but six or seven men stand up and surge to the front of the courtroom. A judge told them they are kings and that he trusts them enough to walk the streets unarmed. A judge told them they are not just part of the problem but part of the solution, too. A judge proved that he sees them as more than simply case numbers on sheets of paper.

They want to thank him for telling them about the Buffalo Soldiers, slain civil rights workers, and the power of men who wear suits and look prepared for business. They also want to thank him for telling them about a thing called honor, something all men and women can claim, even if they fail drug tests, carry shotguns, or fumble famous murder cases. The key to honor is somewhere in this church of a courtroom, in the judge's pleading eyes, in the deputy sheriff's take-no-prisoners' talk, in the half-frightened faces of the four young children whose uncle has brought them to court. The judge says it's up to them to shelter those children from drive-by shooters and debt-collecting dealers. They promise to try.

Betty DeRamus is a lifelong Detroiter and veteran journalist. She has been a reporter and editorial writer for the Detroit Free Press *and the* Michigan Chronicle, *and in 1987 she began writing a column for the Metro section of the* Detroit News. *DeRamus has received dozens of awards, including first prize for education reporting from the Charles Stewart Mott Foundation and the Deems Taylor award from the American Society of Composers, Authors, and Publishers. A recipient of a Eugene Pulliam fellowship for editorial writers, she received the Best of Gannett award four years in a row, and in 1993 was a finalist for the Pulitzer Prize in commentary. Her work has appeared in various publications, including the essay collection* Thinking Black: Some of the Nation's Best Black Columnists Speak Their Minds.

The Dardenilla Dilemma:
Selling Hostile Chocolate and Vanilla Animus
Stanley Crouch

*Now it seemed like Marcia and me against that team of
nine prominent, ruthless lawyers.*
— Christopher Darden, *In Contempt*

*The prosecution of O. J. Simpson was the most incompetent
criminal prosecution I have ever seen. By far. There have
undoubtedly been worse. It's just that I'm not aware of any.*
— Vincent Bugliosi, *Outrage*

We know that in the Montana summer of 1876,
George Armstrong Custer attacked an encampment of
five thousand to ten thousand Indians with three hundred men. Not a good idea. But, until recently, history
did not handle him as it might have. For his astonishing
blunder, one of the worst decisions in all military history,
Custer became a national hero, the symbol of the valiant
leader standing next to the flag of the Seventh Cavalry,
his flaxen hair blowing in the dusty wind, his mustache
and goatee perfectly trimmed, his buckskin jacket hanging as though tailored, his blue eyes showing no fear as
the two six-guns he possessed alternately blasted away
at an endless swarm of bloodthirsty redskins. In dime
novels, on street corners, in office buildings, in front of
fireplaces, at dinner tables, in pool halls, on front

porches, and among schoolchildren, Custer's story was told over and over. Soon, his proportions took on those of a legend; he became emblematic of what the country had to endure to spread the train of its greatness from sea to shining sea. The grit, discipline, spit, and polish of civilization went down before a bunch of whooping savages. It was, however, the last significant victory for the Indians. With the massacre at Little Bighorn memorially ablaze behind their foreheads, American forces went on to crush the hostiles, tribe by tribe, and the governmental bureaucracy conceived of a way to put them in their place. The various representatives of these United States taught them a thing or two. They'd had their day, and it didn't last long.

Now, that irrepressible pony soldier, Old Yellow Hair, the Son of the Morning Star himself, has returned to walk among us multiplied. I say this because what the members of the prosecution team in the O. J. Simpson case want to create for themselves is a Custer's Last Stand of jurisprudence that will allow them a permanent place in the martyrs' pantheon of Americana. They want to become heroes for losing, even though their blunders were substantial enough to make them targets of the kind of scorn athletes receive when they choke during the championship games that conclude the season. This attempt to define themselves demands plenty of ad hominem to take the focus off those errors, which were watched by who knows how many people, both nationally and internationally. If that wasn't enough, hundreds upon hundreds of hours were devoted to analyzing each televised day in court. But there is still a way out. The easiest is to assert that the jurors who decided the outcome were riddled with racial animus or were incapable of assessing complex evidence—or both.

Although this willingness to pass the buck seems true of every member of the prosecution team, one member stands out like a marshmallow in a bowl of chocolate pudding. That one is Christopher A. Darden, the joy of Geraldo Rivera, Charles Grodin, and Dennis Miller, three examples so different that they make it clear why Darden has become a minor celebrity in the wake of the murder trial. Darden's mask of high moral outrage matches theirs, allowing such people to pat themselves on the back at the same time that they commend him for rising above the irrational temptations of racial loyalty and looking at the facts with unconditional courage.

Darden would agree. When he swaggers on screen for a talk show, barely restraining the smile inspired by the introduction and the applause, the former prosecutor seems intent on becoming old Yellow Hair himself. This man wants to be canonized as a deep-thinking martyr even though he made perhaps the two most serious on-the-spot mistakes of the trial. Darden is the one who asked Simpson to put the gloves on. Later, his emotions unexplainably running riot, he used sexual allusions and condescendingly badgered the unwilling witness for the defense, screenwriter Laura Hart McKinney, until she angrily blurted out that Mark Fuhrman had bragged about planting evidence and cover-ups when she used him as a consultant for a movie script about cops. This blunder allowed material to be introduced that Judge Lance Ito had ruled was beyond the scope of the case. (With typical forthrightness, Darden has failed to address the consequences of his cross-examination of Hart in word or print.) Given such decisions, Darden must have well understood how Custer felt when he was surrounded by the deadly results of his last attack.

Along the way, we should not forget that Darden and Marcia Clark exhibited no more shame than the rest who huckstered their relationships to the gore on Bundy Drive. The prosecutors finally responded to the overtures of the agents seeking to represent them and, after quite successful negotiations, each signed a seven-figure book contract that was sealed in the blood of Nicole Brown Simpson and Ronald Goldman. After all, given the billion dollars or more that were generated by the case—expenditures and profits for and from electronic coverage, print coverage, press accommodations, transportation, photographs, souvenirs, investigation by the prosecution as well as the defense, expert witnesses, lawyers, long-distance telephone calls, and so on—why shouldn't a couple of public servants line their pockets? (The greed shown by this pair of prosecutors makes the case that there ought to be a law against public servants writing about their work sooner than ten years after the fact.) Darden and Clark, pressed by tabloid gossip into uncorroborated copulation, made sure they weren't walking home broke after this trial. They intended to have it made in the shade. They weren't only going to morph themselves self-righteously into victims. They would rise rich and famous from the ashes of their defeat, ostentatiously flapping their phoenix wings. Especially Christopher A. Darden.

But Darden's popularity on the talk-show circuit and in the rest of the media is understandable, if only because serious Americans—black, white, or any other color—are anxious to hear straight talk about the latest developments in our racial crisis, especially from Negroes. His intellectual clumsiness notwithstanding, Darden is important to many because he is one of the few in the public eye who seems to distinguish himself from those who rant as loudly as possible about white racism but bite their tongues when subjects like Louis Farrakhan come up, sometimes asserting that they refuse to pass some white-imposed "test" by attacking other black people. What such statements about "required" attacks on Farrakhan actually illustrate is that none of us can improve upon the rationalizations or the passion of the cowardly when it comes to justifying the chicken-hearted nature of their sensibilities. Therefore, Darden is held up by his admirers as the opposite of those Negroes too squeamish to speak their minds and let the truth fall where it may. He keeps their hope alive by representing a return to the fresh, unsentimental assessment of our dilemmas and a rejection of the conventions that embitter racial discourse.

All of this praise for Darden is an audible extension of the usually unspoken reservations many white people have about the racial atmosphere that has developed over the past thirty years. When the Black Power movement arrived in 1966, it rejected fundamental democratic reasoning in favor of tribalism, ethnic self-worship, and the idea that a basic standard of conduct is no more than another version of white supremacy. With Black Power, nearly everything black became good while everything white became if not bad, at least highly suspect. A twisted cultural relativism reared itself. Rooted in the nineteenth-century European disdain for the bourgeoisie and the lower-class American antipathy toward refinement, Black Power railed against "white middle-class standards." If a Negro adhered to what had formally been no more than an expression of class or the expansion of one's taste, he or she was seen as "trying to be white." Ironically, this interpretation was traditionally expressed by the white racists who found any Negro's aspirations beyond hard labor, cooking, dancing, and singing laughable or pretentious or dangerously presumptive. One senator even became famous during the 1970s by saying that all niggers wanted was some loose shoes, some tight hoonyang, and a warm place to take a dump. So if a Negro's aspirations weren't perfect subjects for jokes, that Negro was thought of as "uppity."

None of this, within the context of the Simpson double-murder trial, is separate from the American epic of class hostilities and the tales of ethnic types losing connections to their roots. Simpson's image of success and his change of social context goes right to the center of our country's struggle to understand both our traditional backgrounds and the resistance to our dreams— not to mention our struggle to face the truth that those very dreams might not be insubstantial. In our history and our arts are the many stories of those who have pushed their way up from the bottom and those at the top who have searched down below for a more vibrant relationship to life. But because we fear being or becoming second rate and have so often been disappointed by people from every layer of the social spectrum, we feel equally ambivalent toward the supposed vitality of the poor as we do toward the purported sophistication of the rich. We know that although there may be much chaos at the bottom, there may be just as much at the top. We tire neither of satirically cutting through the sanctimonious camouflage of the yahoos at the bottom nor of ridiculing the spiritual igloos of the upper class. We hate phony baloneys and have made "the real" our holy grail.

It is this combination of ambivalence and cynicism that makes us potential chumps where race, religion, and sex are concerned. We have trouble getting through to the human reality. At our worst, we may try to resolve our conflicts by accepting some demagogue's definition of a "real" Negro, a "real" Jew, a "real" Christian, a "real" Hispanic, a "real" woman, and so on. What the demagogue wants is a following strapped into his bus seats by thick belts of hostility and resentment. Once we are strapped, the demagogue proceeds to tell us where our group identity stops and where our expressions of self-hatred, delusion, and gullibility begin. We are admonished to understand that "beyond this point you are losing connection to us; you are becoming one of them." (Even Vincent Bugliosi falls for this line in *Outrage*, his book about the Simpson trial: "Although Simpson wasn't the classically passive and submissive black* memorialized in Harriet Beecher Stowe's novel *Uncle Tom's Cabin*, he easily fell within the more expansive popular definition of the term—a black who has not only forgotten his roots, but virtually turned his back on the black community, striving to become a white man in every possible way.")

To understand these issues better, one needs to read Arthur Schlesinger Jr.'s discussion in *The Disuniting of America*, one of the most clearly thought-out discussions of our "authenticity blues." Schlesinger observed that America has always been a country of miscegenation, even when miscegenation was largely only the mixing of different nationalities. As he put it: "Those intrepid Europeans who had torn up their roots to brave the wild Atlantic *wanted* to forget a horrid past

---

*Bugliosi's wrong about that, too.

and to embrace a hopeful future. They *expected* to become Americans. Their goals were escape, deliverance, assimilation. They saw America as a transforming nation, banishing dismal memories and developing a unique national character based on common political ideals and shared experiences. The point of America was not to preserve old cultures, but to forge a new *American* culture." Schlesinger then pointed out that the twentieth century brought with it many reservations about assimilation. Assimilation was seen as a technique of oppression, a way of victimizing people by tearing them away from their history.

The mass media's unrelenting attention to the Simpson trial brought all these elements into what most in the profession of law thought should have been, however high profile, a straightforward murder trial, another shocking crime of passion among the rich and famous. On the other hand, Simpson held a special place in our hearts because his was the rags-to-riches tale, and he seemed, in a modest and unpretentious way, to have become the truly American aristocrat, capable of traversing our society and drawing out the better human influences, no matter his point of origin. We now know that Simpson, at the time of the murders, was handsome, charming, violent, and illiterate. His years of fame and coddling had infantilized one side of him. He was a middle-aged, muscular brat who narcissistically prowled through his own paradise with the special arrogance of a celebrity accustomed to universal deference. But there are also those who are outraged by the fact that Simpson didn't make Negro social causes priorities in his life, as though he was required to—which he was not. The man had benefited from the disciplined development of his athletic prowess, not from anything particular to Afro-American culture of the sort that so many musicians, actors, dancers, and writers have built their reputations on, none of whom, by the way, are obligated to become crusaders for the race or philanthropists. He had the right to live as he chose, marrying whom he wished and socializing according to his own preferences. Yet, there was the rub. As the prime suspect in two grisly murders picked over by the media, Simpson was still black, widely loved, and on trial in Los Angeles, where racial tensions have exploded every few years in the 1990s.

That is where Christopher A. Darden comes in. The man many assumed was brought aboard to mitigate the negative impression of a famous black man being prosecuted for murder by an all-white team, Darden is neither simple nor easily dismissed. But he is truly a son of his era. *In Contempt*, his autobiography and his version of the Simpson case, unintentionally reveals that Darden has a rather confused vision of the difference between social determinism and individual choice. He is, therefore, both a perfect Californian and a perfect sore loser. In essence, what we get from Darden's book is another spin on the victim vision. Ours is a time in which we should expect such things and, in some ways, it is fitting that the conspiracy theory of the defense, which portrayed the wealthy Simpson as a victim of ruthless law-enforcement hanky-panky and racism, has now been countered by a theory in which the prosecution, the jury system, and the very law itself have been victimized by some irrational colored people. Darden's excuse is familiar because it is the same one used for so many other kinds of failure—"It wasn't me. Somebody did it to me. I'm sitting here facing accusations because of forces beyond my control. I never got an even break. I got off the bench with two strikes against me. Oh, one more thing: Society didn't help me to stack up enough self-esteem for me to act the way I *should* act. I've been had, up, down, and around and around." In Darden's own words, "We were prosecutors, civil servants, and not rich, powerful lawyers." Poor kids.

At the center of this controversy is the question of whether or not one's actions can yet be assessed on individual terms—especially when the stakes are as high as the stakes ever get. Was it possible for O. J. Simpson to be an individual first and a Negro either second or only incidentally? Was it possible for a predominantly black jury to be a gathering of individual experiences and perspectives instead of largely a mass of Pavlovian darkies ready to drool in unison at the opportunity to vent revenge on a legal system demonstrably mottled by racism? This question sets up the next one: How important is one's ethnic group to what happens in a court of law? Are we so trapped in allegiances to skin color, religion, and culture that justice has a hard time ever appearing in our system? Do we accept extremely limited ideas about "authenticity" that lead us to certain equally reductive conclusions when we are in the midst of an experience, not something we have been told about ourselves? Were Simpson and the jurors contemporary examples of how successfully the ignorant, the brutal, the xenophobic, and the provincial have resisted the complex and the sophisticated?

These are the questions that completely confuse Darden, who can't, for the life of him, understand the problems that obsession with "race" and "culture" have wrought in our society. If Darden is the victim of anything, it is the body of assumptions he has accepted about what makes him who he is and what makes others who they are. He is far from a racist, but is certainly biased, having bought into insubstantial ideas about "African heritage" long ago. Those ideas are indicative of how shallow his understanding is of this country, however many hard, shocking experiences his job has given him. After making the point that "My law school diploma wasn't a black Juris Doctorate," he goes on to write, "I am a lawyer," then comes home with this shiner:

> And I am black. In fact, I love the color of my skin. It is dark and perfect. When you look at me, you don't see the remnants of slavery—light skin, thin lips, pinched nose. You see an African face. I am proud of that.

Darden apparently has no idea how many dark-skinned Negro Americans have both white and Indian ancestors. He has accepted a simple idea about identity, one based equally on "feel-good" propaganda and a rhetorical cliché popularized by Malcolm X during his time with the Nation of Islam. (This reveals Darden's troubled "double consciousness" as a black man who sees himself as standing above the racial divisions in the interest of justice, but who is anxious to assert his recognition of "blackness." Although in his book, he later attacks Johnnie Cochran for calling some white cops "devils," the Nation of Islam's xenophobic name for all whites, Darden, ever befuddled, talks out of both sides of his mouth when he defines the same racist cult both as "a strong, proud, and worthy group [and] . . . the very symbol of black separatism.") Darden heard the following "historical" genealogy from an admired black-studies professor at San Jose State University:

> You are the direct descendants of kings and queens. They didn't load just anyone on those slave ships. They stole only the best and they stole only the brightest. They took the strongest physically and mentally. They took royalty, and that's why you are the sons and daughters of kings and queens. You are the princes and princesses of Africa.

Apparently, this poor Darden believes that there were enough kingdoms on the West Coast of Africa to be split among the millions who were sold into this hemisphere as chattel slaves! Maybe they meant, back in good old Africa, a man's home is his castle. Perhaps Huey Long was passing for white when he spoke of "every man a king." One never knows. Then there is the "brightness" question. Does Darden think that the Africans who captured members of rival tribes gave those other Africans intelligence tests before marching them to the coastal beaches, where they were sold to Europeans? Doesn't he know that those in slavery were seen as no more than livestock by their fellow Africans, the Europeans, and the Arabs who made the nasty business of slavery truly "multicultural"? (It is interesting to note that Darden's charge that the Dream Team exploited race was foreshadowed in the mass media years earlier by Simpson playing the part of an African in paradise who was killed as the whites began scooping up slaves in the first episode of the television miniseries *Roots*. That miniseries was based on a despicably fraudulent work that cashed in on the Black Power appetite for African ancestry, the gold mines of white guilt, and the sob stories of black-studies courses, which were far more often about indoctrination than scholarship.)

In addition to his faulty cultural assumptions, Darden is also controlled by a system of resentment that functions on two tiers, one in which racial misgivings are joined by a stew of anger that mixes—in separate but equal parts—class, luxury, privilege, and reputation. Darden unknowingly reveals one of his central concerns when he writes of his classmates in law school who were from Princeton, Yale, Berkeley, and Stanford:

"These guys with their huge egos and $80,000 educa-
tions were always posturing and posing and doing their
best not to talk to me." At another point in the book,
our genetically untrammeled African complains about
how much leeway celebrities are given in Los Angeles.
Early in the trial he sulks, "It was funny; I was probably
the only lawyer in the room who wasn't famous." But
later, when he becomes a cap-pistol celebrity, our lawyer
with the pure, Gold Coast face observes, "Marcia and I
were being recognized in more and more places. We
were invited to parties where movie stars lined up to
meet *us*. . . . Movie stars and other celebrities are, as a
group, shorter than you'd think. Nicer too." Darden gets
so tangled up in celebrity and the courtroom as a place
of public performance that he refers to the press coverage as good or bad "reviews." The obsessive attention
filled this boy's head with helium, and he floated away.

In this context, when our prosecutor looks at
Simpson's defense—"the whole Dream Team"—and
expresses his resentment with such a vengeance, we
observe a variation on the way Darden felt at law
school when he was surrounded by guys with Ivy
League pedigrees: "I wondered what the criteria could
be for admittance to this team. Among the frontline
attorneys, the only thing they seemed to have in common was their penchant for defending spoiled, nasty
rich people and their ability to attract and create publicity." In his book, Darden calls the defense team all
sorts of names and even referred to F. Lee Bailey as

"foul-mouthed," though he frequently quotes Marcia
Clark using expletives casually, angrily, and affection-
ately. Darden became furious when Cochran, whom he
blames for alienating him from the Afro-American
community, attacked him for asking a witness if he
heard an unseen man with a "black" voice:

> "I resent that statement," Cochran clipped, leaning on
> the podium in his off-white linen suit, like some angry
> plantation owner. "You can't tell by somebody's voice
> whether they sound black."
> His upper lip curled underneath his mustache and
> Cochran came at me again. "That's a racist statement!"

Speaking to the reader, Darden justifies his questions
by reasoning that entertainers "have long fought for the
opportunity to reflect genuine black voices—urban,
hip, with traces of the South, of the West Indies, of
Africa." The poor prosecutor doesn't understand that
region, class, and style, not color, determine whether
one sounds "white" or "black." He should tune in to one
of the talk shows, turn his back, and listen. He will find
something out: In today's world, with so many white
kids and young adults, from the lower to the middle
class, taking their leads from rap, black comedians, and
so on, what was once heard as "black" may now be no
more than another stylistic aspect of Americana, neither a birthright nor a stop sign.

These sorts of confusions on Darden's part only
obscure the far more important subject, which is

whether a murderer slipped through the grip of the legal system. Darden is quite critical of that legal system and believes that the black jurors were sufficiently embittered by how it functions that, when constantly goaded by Cochran, they chose to acquit Simpson. This belief fails to explain how the non-Negro members of the jury—including a strong-willed older white woman whom many pundits expected to hang the jury—were brought aboard for the ride. It uses the excuse of social determinism to mitigate an unpleasant reality. That reality includes a major prosecution witness—a cop— caught lying on the stand. As Darden well knows, such a catastrophe almost automatically leads to acquittal. The reason is simple and obvious, however many mountains of other evidence are on display: Juries, no matter their color, distrust any prosecution team that will bring a lying cop to the stand, put him at the center of its case, speak to him sweetly, and then attack him as contemptuous vermin when the covers are pulled by the defense. Darden's sociological excuse, however self-serving, is an example of the difficulty we have in seeing the legal and penal systems with the clarity that will allow us to recognize the present criminal crisis yet remain on the lookout for those infringements that allow prejudice to tip the scales unfairly against the innocent.

Here is where the complexity comes in. Even if we accept the idea that the justice system unfairly tilts punishment toward lower-class black defendants and that the penal system imprisons a disproportionate number of convicted black men, we have to wonder what this idea actually means when we balance it against the equally disproportionate number of murders, rapes, robberies, and assaults that black people suffer at the hands of other black people who reside in the same communities. The yearly body counts extend far beyond what they were in even the most brutal periods of redneck Southern rule and Northern race riots. The murder and violence have created a racially based national health crisis. The odds that so many young black men will die from violent attacks are not the result of a grim increase in skinheads or Aryan militias bent on race war and genocide. For all the talk of institutional racism—which should be rooted out whenever and wherever its existence can be proved—we haven't developed reasonable emergency policies that are sufficiently stern to intimidate the bulk of those with thug inclinations into adopting civilized behavior. (As one who believes we have to face the best we may actually get, I'll settle for good behavior, not psychological rehabilitation or changing a polluted heart into a pure one. These criminals can think or feel whatever they like as long as they keep a collar on the destructive actions that introduced them to law enforcement. Get a job, act civilized, and purge your anarchic fantasies at the movies.)

As a black prosecutor, Darden earned his living and made whatever reputation he had in that world—before the Simpson case. It is one of the most difficult positions in American society because those who are sympathetic to the collective sense of racial injustice, black or white, are vulnerable to manipulation by the shrewdest lawyers or criminals among us. This vulnerability was discovered in the late 1960s, when the lawyer Charles Gary defended Black Panthers like the murderous Huey Newton. Gary's technique was largely to ignore the charges and put the society on trial. Since then, a trickle-down effect has set in. Now the manipulative lawyer and guilty black criminal can cite slavery, segregation, lynchings, police brutality, prejudiced judges, white juries, and the poverty born of the racism instituted in poor schooling. Last, but in no way the least, there is the lack of a "level playing field," which guarantees low achievement. So the guilty black criminal, when sufficiently crafty, benefits from the unarguable rap sheet that documents thousands of instances of crimes against democratic fairness. (Critics cite the defense of Simpson as a variation on this ploy.)

When this kind of thinking is unsentimentally examined, however, one finds a serious flaw: Crimes past do not erase crimes present, unless one accepts the idea that society is so much stronger than the individual that what we see as crimes could easily be the result of the deformations born of prejudice and deprivation. The logic of this argument is that those who exist outside the circles of privilege are driven mad (at least, temporarily) by bitterness, frustration, and the desperate responses to alienation that form an entire code of behavior, one in which values are often turned upside down. In essence, it is a variation on the insanity defense: The individual is not responsible for his or her actions. Anarchic behavior becomes the most harrowing expression of the alienated, those who feel abandoned because of their color and their poverty.

Although such arguments may work among the tenderhearted, especially those who are well educated enough to have had their brains stewed in sociology and psychoanalysis, the people on the receiving end of the actions of predators don't feel much sympathy for them. The victims are educated in statistics covered by bruises and fresh blood. Their opinions are outside the realms of the academy, where life remains the same whether or not the theorists are right. Those Negro Americans who know crime from the receiving end argue that many people aren't doing as well as they would like, but that doesn't make it right or acceptable to destroy the feeling of safety and freedom in a community. Those Negro Americans are as bent on law and order as you can get. Whereas some others may whine about the police presence and claim unnecessary harassment, these black people certainly don't support the excesses of law enforcement, but they do want *more* police and stronger police action. They want the streets cleared of criminals and, as one woman in a New Jersey housing project said, "I don't care whether they put them in the jail, behind the jail, or under the jail. All I want is for them to be gone out of here."

Darden, who prosecuted violent criminals, from murdering gang members to mad serial killers, came to know the meaning of that attitude. In 1985, he was part of a special unit organized to "hit gangs hard, to coordinate prosecution and specifically target the young men involved in the drug trade, in the random robberies and constant murders of gang life." That year there were 271 gang murders; six years later, there were more than 700. Darden saw convincingly vivid examples of what these people had done to their communities:

> I drove home at night through neighborhoods in various states of warfare with gangs, some in which the families were held captive behind barred windows because of packs of fifteen-year-olds with semi-automatic weapons; other neighborhoods in which the families just gave up and moved farther away and the houses, the duplexes, and apartments dissolved into bullet-pocked crack houses and shooting galleries.

In 1988, Darden went to work in the Special Investigation Division, "where public officials, primarily police officers, were investigated for the crimes they might have committed." Darden learned why many people were terrified of the police:

> In SID, I quickly found out there was plenty of reason to be afraid. There was a small percentage of cops so dirty, you couldn't imagine a crime they hadn't committed. The files fell onto our desks like dirty snow—rape, embezzlement, fraud, theft, bribery, intimidation,

blackmail, assault, even homicide. And that same bunker mentality, that code of silence, allowed them to get away with it more often than other criminals.

So when Darden was brought on the prosecution team for the Simpson trial, he had seen the casualties wrought by both sides of the sword, those cut down by minority criminals and those done harm by dirty cops. That is why he believes that the system itself is at least partially responsible for black Americans' attitudes toward law enforcement, both the courts and the cop on the street. While Darden has no trouble recognizing a race strategy in court, in his book, he dons the victim's cloak and works so hard to burn Johnnie Cochran at the stake that analysis disappears in the smoke of attempted revenge and self-inflation:

> Cochran had decided that everything in this case would be racial strategy and the pundits were playing right along, buying into that hype. . . . Everything in this case was sifted through a filter of bigoted expectations, like the pressure Jackie Robinson faced when he broke the color barrier in baseball. "Pretty good hitter for a darkie." It was bad for our case, but it was worse for the country. We were being ratcheted back fifty years because of a lying, murdering ex-jock and his unprincipled legal team. And the media, the pundits, and the starstruck judge played gleefully along.

Though Darden sneers at the idea that Simpson, "a millionaire who was given every deference by the sys-

tem," would have the nerve to allow the factual suffer-
ing of black people to be used as an abstract shield for
his murders, he doesn't flinch when comparing himself
to Jackie Robinson! He also says: "It was our responsibility to try to appeal to this group of people, no matter
how suspicious and bitter they were. And we failed. But
I would rather fail than win by perverting and twisting
the justice system—as I believe the defense team did."
This is whining of the worst sort. It is not possible for a
defense team to pervert and twist our system of justice
unless it pays off judges, jurors, and witnesses. Cochran
and his crew did nothing of the sort. They raised reasonable doubts that the jury swallowed.

I also do not believe we were pushed back to any earlier point in American racial history by the jury's verdict in the Simpson case. Those who found the verdict
incomprehensible or thought it proof of Negro stupid-
ity weren't about to think much of Negroes anyway. Or
they would have figured out how to explain why
exceptional Negroes outside athletics weren't representative of their group—genetic flukes of no consequence
to the fundamental and endless inferiority. It is also true
that since the most popular people in America are
probably Colin Powell, Michael Jordan, and Oprah
Winfrey, we don't seem to have lost much ground
because of a hypnotic murder trial. Not one of these
people seemed to lose a single white admirer after the
verdict was read. The real issue, as Bugliosi pointed out
in his book, *Outrage*, is that the prosecution completely

screwed up its own case by not presenting stronger evidence, not providing sufficient counterarguments to the defense, and not having an overall strategy that would have made use of what Darden said was essential: "Never in our legal system has so much blood and DNA evidence been amassed against one defendant." The members of the prosecution team were not fallen heroes undone by a justice system that had been unscrupulously devastated by the out-of-order issue of race. Bugliosi took into consideration the limitations and potential prejudices of the jury but stated that Simpson could still have been convicted by the same twelve people who acquitted him. So the greatest disservice to Nicole Brown Simpson and Ronald Goldman was not the Dream Team but the prosecution itself. When all the sentiment from either side is removed, one thing is clear: The prosecution was not up to the job.

That fact makes the murder trial a double tragedy, given our national unwillingness to recognize ineptitude. We allow even the George Armstrong Custers of our day to cover themselves in martyred glory because we would rather kiss the putrid wounds of these public servants than face the fact that those stinking wounds were self-inflicted.

Stanley Crouch *is an award-winning writer whose work has appeared in the* New York Times, Vogue, Harper's, *and*

The New Yorker. *A staff writer for the* Village Voice *for nine years, he is currently a contributing editor at the* New Republic *and a columnist for the* New York Daily News. *His collections of essays,* The All-American Skin Game *and* Notes of a Hanging Judge, *were both nominated for awards in criticism by the National Book Critics Circle. Mr. Crouch is the artistic consultant for jazz programming at New York City's Lincoln Center and is a founder of Jazz at Lincoln Center.*

Joe Frazier for the Prosecution

ELLIS COSE

Johnnie Cochran is no Muhammad Ali, and Christopher Darden is no Joe Frazier. Still, there are certain similarities between the so-called trial of the century and the Ali-Frazier war—the three bitter, heart-stopping battles that spanned four years and left both gladiators hallowed as heroes, depleted as fighters, and, in some respects, diminished as men. "It was like death. Closest thing to dyin' that I know of," Ali confessed after the hellishly brutal final brawl, the one staged in Manila, in which he rallied valiantly in the fourteenth round and ultimately prevailed. Frazier, who fought the last rounds nearly blind, finished in no better condition. Each boxer left a substantial part of himself in the ring.

Yet as bad as was the damage to the fighters' bodies, the suffering was not merely physical. At stake, as Ali had made clear from the beginning, was not merely a heavyweight title. In the eyes of much of the public—and certainly in his own eyes—Ali was a warrior with an epic calling. "My mission is to bring freedom to thirty million black people," Ali had declared at one point. In contrast, Frazier had no cause—except perhaps that of being a turncoat, a tool of a repugnant system. Given all that hung in the balance—no less than liberation for thirty million souls—Frazier's utter humiliation was essential. So Ali made a point of ridiculing both the fighter and the man, designating him an ignoramus, a gorilla, and, perhaps worst of all, an Uncle Tom. Whereas Ali was the "people's champion," Frazier was the white man's boy—a tool of the system and an enemy of his people whose success would forevermore be tainted by the accusation of racial treachery.

Frazier took the disparagement personally (since there was no other way to take it), and to this day, according to all accounts, he harbors a bitterness toward Ali that he will carry to his grave. (Reflecting on Ali's ceremonial lighting of the torch for the 1996 Olympics, Frazier told a Philadelphia newspaper columnist, "If I would have been on the platform with him, I would have thrown him into the flame.") For Ali, by casting him as an Uncle Tom, ensured that Frazier would have the fight of his life, and one that (even though he triumphed in the initial bout in 1971) he could never truly win. It is, after all, virtually impossible to prevail over a vague suspicion of moral complicity, over innuendo and specious charges—accusations that even as they disparage the target, illuminate the cruelty of the taunter, yet are no less durable for being false.

Cochran, to repeat the point, is no Ali. Yet, in his attempt to demolish Darden's credibility and undermine his standing in "the community," Cochran cast himself in a comparably heroic role. Like Ali, he had a higher goal. He was not merely fighting for one rich man's freedom but leading a grand "journey to justice," a momentous odyssey that would end in an American Eden with the creation of a more perfect union. "If you don't speak out, if you don't stand up, if you don't do what's right," he warned the jury with absolute self-assurance, "this kind of conduct will continue on forever. And we'll never have an ideal society."

In pursuit of that goal—or at least what Cochran *claimed* to be that goal—the defense apparently deemed that discrediting Darden was no less essential than Ali thought denigrating Frazier would be. So Darden was designated an Uncle Tom, a collaborator with the white man and his bigoted system. In his book, *In Contempt*, Darden confessed to wondering during Cochran's summation whether he himself was on trial. And, certainly, in some sense, he was. For somehow the Simpson trial became so much more than a simple legal determination of whether a rich celebrity, former athlete, and known wife beater had snapped and killed his former spouse and her friend. It became, among other things, a debate about different views of blackness, about whether blacks can afford the luxury of placing much faith in a "white" system of justice, and about whether those who participate in that system—or, at least, those who endeavor to put fellow blacks in jail by working as prosecutors—are worthy of membership in the black race. It also became, as Cochran so stirringly pointed out to the jury, a way to send a potent message, to hold America symbolically accountable for the racism and brutality of the police, for the untold atrocities and indignities visited on blacks across the years for daring to demand basic human courtesies: "Maybe you're the right people, at the right time, at the right place to say, 'No more—we're not going to have this.'"

The problem with symbolism, however, is that it is often rooted in little more than fantasy (or worse, lies). Consequently, symbolic victories, for the most part, do not so much represent the defeat of real enemies as the triumph of imagination over logic and common sense.

As journalist Isabel Wilkerson grimly observed in *Essence* magazine: "Whatever the facts, many of us have been so hungry for a savior, so tired of being on the losing side of America's race war that we see Malcolm and Martin and the Scottsboro boys in every Black man who comes under public (read White) attack." Yet the reality is that the outcome of America's racial war could no more be decided in this era by Simpson than it could, in an earlier age, have been by Ali.

Ali, great fighter that he always was and globally revered icon and humanitarian that he eventually

became, did not—for all his magnificence in and outside the ring—liberate thirty million people. And
Cochran did not bring America one step closer to being
a more "ideal society." He certainly got his celebrity
client off, which is what he was paid to do, and made
himself more celebrated in the process. But he never
even remotely established that Simpson's acquittal was
a victory for black America, or, for that matter, that it
was of the slightest benefit to any community of any
color—other, perhaps, than the community of
Simpson's friends and fans. Yet, Cochran managed to
convince much of his audience (which was obviously
much larger than the jury) that somehow Simpson's
success was a triumph for the larger community and
that in battling Simpson, Darden had been at war with
blackness itself.

Near the end of his memoir of the Simpson trial,
Darden described a tribute to him in Los Angeles at
which he responded to Cochran's gibe, made in the
presence of television cameras, that Cochran looked
forward to welcoming Darden "back to the community." Well after the trial was over, Cochran's words continued to haunt Darden, in the same way that Ali's
seemed to have haunted Frazier. So Darden, at the tribute and in the book, answered with practiced contempt: "You don't have to welcome me back into the
community, because I never left." Yet even Darden
seems less than entirely certain that he is still a member
of that community in good standing. "Perhaps I had to

be 'kicked out' of the black community," he mused, "to understand my place in it." He wrote of the strange twilight zone "between black perception and white perception" to which he was transported during the trial. And he wrote as well, and evidently with a sense of deep regret, of the "Darden Dilemma," the pressure felt by black prosecutors "for standing up and convicting black criminals."

In an interview with William Claiborne, a staff writer for the *Washington Post*, Darden expanded on his thoughts: "There is a dilemma, and one wonders whether one is misusing or abusing one's talents. Assuming that I'm a talented lawyer, should I be using that talent to send black men to prison? When I leave the courthouse at the end of the day, I go back to that same community where the twenty-five defendants I ran into . . . that day live. In a sense, I live where I work." Though Darden was still convinced that it was necessary for blacks to remain in the system, that they added a dimension of compassion and understanding that otherwise would be lacking, he was not convinced that he wished to continue to be a part of it.

For anyone even vaguely familiar with the statistics on incarceration, Darden's shakiness is understandable, for those statistics add up to a stunning statement about the racially disparate impact of the enforcement of America's laws. A black man's odds of being incarcerated are nearly eight times a white man's, according to the U.S. Department of Justice. Black women, though incarcerated in substantially smaller numbers than black men, are incarcerated at seven times the rate of white women. And the statistics will almost certainly get worse. As any number of demographers have pointed out, the population of young black, and Hispanic, males (specifically teens and young adults) is growing much faster than the population of young white males, and it is young males, more than any other segment of the population, who tend to get into trouble with the law. The future of a large part of the black community, in short, is a future to be spent largely behind bars—unless something dramatic happens to change things. And, as Darden is well aware, there are precious few signs of systemic change for the better on the horizon.

The Sentencing Project, a Washington-based non-profit group, has garnered a lot of publicity in recent years by publishing statistics documenting the growth and extent of the incarceration of blacks. In 1990, the organization released a study noting that nearly one in four black men aged twenty to twenty-nine was in prison or jail or on probation or parole. By 1995, the figure had grown to 32.2 percent. The project's 1995 report concluded: "If the goal of public policy in recent years had been to incarcerate record numbers of black Americans, then that policy would have been a tremendous success. But if the goal was to make our streets safer and to build strong families and communities, then public policy has been a dramatic failure."

Even without the ever-increasing number of black prisoners, many blacks would be leery of the justice system for no other reasons than those inculcated by their own experience, for it's hard to find any black adult in America who has not had an unpleasant encounter with the law, who has not been stopped, for instance, by disrespectful police spoiling for a fight or perhaps a bit too eager to assert their authority over members of a race they view indiscriminately as a threat to the civil order.

In the March 1996 issue of the *Washington Monthly*, Joseph Kennedy, a black Washington-area resident, described two separate occasions when his two adult sons were wrongly picked up by the police. One was suspected of robbing a woman, and the other was accused of assaulting a policeman, but in Kennedy's eyes, their real crimes were that they were black men in the wrong neighborhood. Although, in both cases, the wrongs were eventually set right, the encounters left Kennedy embittered and in distress. In summing up his experience with his son who was falsely accused of attacking a police officer, Kennedy wrote:

In the end, the system won. Our lawyers advised us to accept a financial settlement as well as an agreement that the police academy would revise any racially stereotypical training materials. We settled because we knew the proceedings could go on indefinitely. The county could wear us down financially. . . . While numerous brutality complaints had been filed in

Arlington County in the past, no case had ever been won. We were the first. After 18 months, the ordeal that began on an early Sunday morning was over. But the arrest of our two sons, the long, drawn-out helplessness and pain, the feeling that a lifetime of family values and beliefs were being questioned, the anger that my sons faced prison terms simply because of their skin color, cannot be forgotten. Neither can I forget that because we are black, it could all happen again.

Kennedy's opinion is by no means rare among blacks and is not without foundation—as even some hard-core defenders of the justice system will acknowledge. John J. Dilulio Jr., a political scientist at Princeton University and an outspoken proponent of aggressive incarceration, conceded that "blacks really do experience enough casual, reflexive racism from law enforcement officers to make them understandably fearful that racism permeates the criminal justice system." Dilulio argued, however, that the perception is wrong. In "My Black Crime Problem, and Ours," his provocatively entitled article in the Spring 1996 issue of the *City Journal*, Dilulio asserted:

> The bottom line of most of the best research is that America's justice system is *not* racist, not anymore, not as it undoubtedly was a generation ago. . . . If blacks are overrepresented in the ranks of the imprisoned, it is because blacks are overrepresented in the criminal ranks—and the violent criminal ranks, at that. Yes, there are ways in which the justice system is failing all Americans, including black Americans. But to the

extent that the justice system hurts, rather than helps, blacks more than it does white, it is not by incarcerating a "disproportionate" number of black men. Rather, it is by ignoring poor black victims and letting convicted violent and repeat black criminals, both adult and juvenile, continue to victimize and demoralize the black communities that suffer most of their depredations.

No group occupies a more delicate position in the debate about black criminals versus black victims than do beleaguered black prosecuting attorneys. Black prosecutors know the statistics as well as anyone; they also know, more intimately than most, the faces—and the records—behind the numbers. And many of the prosecutors, as Darden concluded, do indeed find themselves torn. They worry about the consequences of putting so many black men in prison. Yet they also acknowledge Dilulio's point that black communities suffer the most from black criminals, and they wonder about the consequences of letting people go free who have shown, usually repeatedly, that they will prey on others without restraint or remorse if given the opportunity. As Paul Gamble, an assistant U.S. attorney in New York observed, "I don't think Martin Luther King Jr. would say, 'Give the brother a break, even though he robbed or murdered someone.'"

Yet, if someone doesn't "give the brother a break," what are the implications for the future of black America? Are we prepared to accept the possibility that the only appropriate place for perhaps a third of young black men is on a conveyor belt to jail en route to hell? And even if many blacks do belong in jail, should black lawyers have anything to do with sending them there?

Darden is hardly alone in pondering the answers to such questions. A black graduate of an Ivy League law school, not yet thirty, who now works as a big-city prosecutor, said the questions arose for him even before he left law school. After accepting the prosecutor's position, he began to wonder whether he was a sellout, the concern sown, in large measure, by comments from classmates who disapproved of his choice of a career. Even among some elders to whom he looked for guidance, his decision was not well received. A well-known black law professor whom he had long admired scolded him for accepting the position. "All you're going to be doing," said the older man, "is putting brothers in jail." Even if blacks were guilty, the professor seemed to be saying, it was not the business of other blacks to put them in the white man's prison. The comment, made several years ago, still hurts, for it seemed to question the student's racial integrity. His relationship with the professor, confided his former student, was never quite the same after the stinging—if subtle—accusation. Some of his sense of closeness to and respect for the older man vanished. Nonetheless, the young prosecutor said, he took the job because, having worked a summer in a prosecutor's office, he thought he could do some good and realized he had some discretion in how he carried out his assignments. "If I honestly believe someone is innocent," he pointed out, "I have the ability to dismiss a case." Moreover, he thinks it is wrong to let those who rob, kill, and rape walk away from their crimes without penalty. "I don't think I'm going to solve the world's problems in my job, but I think I can help out, in some minor way, by holding some people responsible for their actions," he explained.

This is not to say that black prosecutors don't see discrimination and injustices in the system. Indeed, those injustices sometimes move them to despair. "It's very hard when you look across the table at someone who could be your brother, or even your husband, and you realize they could go to jail for a long, long time," confided Marcia Cooke, executive assistant U.S. attorney for the South Florida district. Cooke is particularly bothered by sentencing laws that mandate much stiffer penalties for possession of crack cocaine than for powder cocaine. Those laws are a large part of the reason why whites (who are more likely to be arrested for possessing powder cocaine) often are convicted of misdemeanors while blacks (who are more likely to be caught with crack) are found guilty of felonies and draw stiff prison sentences. Under mandatory sentencing guidelines, for instance, a defendant who is caught with one gram of crack cocaine could end up serving the same amount of time as someone caught with one hundred grams of powder. Just over five grams of crack might mean a sentence of five years without parole, while five grams of powder would likely result in probation. Yet, even when confronted with such blatant disparities, some black prosecutors find solace in the fact that the system is more equitable because they take part in it. "At least if you have a black prosecutor in there, there's some semblance of fairness," commented Patricia Gatling, an executive assistant district attorney in Brooklyn who specializes in drug prosecutions. Yet even Gatling, a former president of the National Black Prosecutors Association, acknowledges that the role played by black prosecutors is not widely appreciated and that the lack of community support takes a toll. "Sometimes we sort of feel, 'Are we really doing any good here?' because no one's out there cheering us," she said.

Jeffrey Craig, deputy attorney general of Pennsylvania, remarked that the disapproval in his own community can be so intense as to be painful. "Sometimes I'm very apprehensive about even telling black people what I do." For though he tries always to conduct himself in an honorable way, he does not expect people to see past the stereotype, and though he prosecutes primarily white-collar crimes and most of his defendants are white, he knows that people won't recognize that fact from his job title. Nor will they understand that he is a critic of a system that, at times, especially when it deals with petty criminals, ends up "putting a bandage on an infected sore." The general public, he realizes, has no way of knowing that he goes out of his way to be fair to black defendants, that he shares many of the experiences they have had, and that he bristles, just as they do, at any hint of police misconduct. All his critics know, or think they know, said Craig, is that "I'm a turncoat, that I'm not helping my brothers and sisters." They see him, in short, as "part of the assembly line of degradation and oppression of black people."

As a former cop, Craig is accustomed to being shunned—even feared—by fellow blacks. Yet, the rejection clearly pains him—as it does a number of other black prosecutors—even though those I have talked to, without exception, believe the system works better with them than it would without them. The problem, they noted, comes when defense lawyers and black defendants expect them to look the other way when blacks commit serious crimes or to make excuses for behavior that is simply inexcusable. Odell McGhee, an assistant district attorney in Polk County, Iowa, said that some defense lawyers saw it as his job to "give them the break no one else will give them." Because he has refused to give in to such pressure, McGhee contended, the minority defense bar has blocked his ambition to become a judge. "I've become very discouraged sometimes when I try to do a good job," he admitted.

Cooke, the Florida prosecutor, said that she, too, has felt discouraged. "Intellectually you're doing the right thing, but the emotional response can be very different." When young black prosecutors come into her office to share their frustration, she advises them that the pain of watching countless black men being locked up comes with the job. The most important thing they can do, she tells them, is to "make certain you're a righteous prosecutor," in other words, that they make the extra effort to ensure that blacks—victims as well as defendants—are not abused by the system.

Again and again, when black prosecutors are asked about their work, they describe themselves as a check on a system that, left to its own, is extremely hostile to minorities, a system that routinely assumes the worst whenever it encounters black people. Knowing that, some minority prosecutors consider it essential to make distinctions that cops might not make or to grill policemen more closely than is the norm. Even though Gatling is a staunch antidrug crusader, for instance, she can be extremely tough on police officers who swarm into predominantly minority communities and arrest people indiscriminately. Part of her job, she believes, is to make a difference, which sometimes means that she criticizes things that a white prosecutor might let go.

Indeed, when condemned as race traitors or Uncle Toms, some black prosecutors (as well as judges and police officers) indignantly inquire whether their critics would prefer that the system be all white. After all, only in the past three decades have blacks been permitted to enter the system in significant numbers—and the vast majority of prosecutors, judges, and other court officers continue to be white. And as Bruce Wright (who served several years as a criminal-court judge in New York City) observed, that color scheme can create some obvious problems of its own. In *Black Robes White Justice*, his book about his experiences in the justice system, Wright wrote: "My persistent concern has long been the white judges, who, in large numbers, are called upon daily to preside over the trials of black defendants accused of crime. Are they qualified for such sociological tasks, only incidentally mixed with law? . . . What do they study in college or law school that qualifies them to decide the doom or liberty of strangers to their neighborhoods, aliens to their way of life, foreigners and outsiders to their clubs, their churches, their synagogues, their history, their work, their culture, and their folkways?" Wright resolved that in his own courtroom, he would see to it that "neither white skin nor black skin would be discriminated against." His efforts to pursue his concept of fairness, particularly for defendants, won him the opprobrium of the Patrolmen's Benevolent Association, which thought he set bails too low and was too eager to set criminals free and dubbed him "Turn 'em Loose Bruce." In a 1995 interview with *Newsday*, Wright said he never took offense at the nickname: "It became a term of affection in the black sections of the city. . . . It has attracted people who said they loved me and wanted to protect me. It's a warm feeling to be addressed as 'Turn 'em Loose Bruce,' especially here in Harlem."

It is not surprising that prosecutors tend to identify most closely with victims, not defendants, for they also know that when it comes to violent crimes, blacks are among the most victimized. For instance, over 50 percent of all murder victims in the United States are black, as are roughly 40 percent of children aged twelve and under who are murdered. Often, when the killing or violent assault is over, it is up to the prosecutor to help the survivor or the victim pick up the pieces. "If it makes a victim feel better that I'm there," Gatling said, then so much the better. Victims, prosecutors believe, need protection from the predators in their midst at least as much as predators need protection from the hostile justice system.

Indeed, the reason many prosecutors went into their line of work was not out of some perverted desire to lock up black men, but out of a sincere aspiration to do something worthwhile with their lives, to perform some kind of public service from which their communities would benefit. In fact, some black prosecutors, like Darden and Gatling, spent much of their early careers prosecuting brutal cops. Others went south to take on white politicians who were attempting to deny blacks the vote or white peace officers who were trying to deny blacks their civil rights. Others took on high-profile cases of whites who had persecuted blacks. Richard Mangum, executive assistant district attorney in the Bronx, New York, and head of the National Black Prosecutors Association, was on the team that convicted several whites in 1987 of a racist and fatal assault on a black man in Howard Beach.

Yet, as Mangum pointed out, black prosecutors do not have the luxury to pick and choose, to demand only to be assigned cases for which they will clearly be—in the eyes of the black community—on the side of the angels. To accept the calling of a prosecutor, he believes, is to accept the possibility that you will be called on, at times, to try a case that is not popular with the public or to prosecute a defendant who is beloved or admired. It is to accept, in short, the fact that glory does not necessarily come with the job.

In fact, prosecutors are not generally perceived as terribly admirable figures, whatever their race. In popular culture, prosecutors are often the bad guys—mean-spirited, soulless bureaucrats who are dedicated to making life worse for everyone. As Hollywood sees them, they either let go crooks who are collared by the Dirty Harrys of the world on the basis of technicalities, or they try to send people to jail (think of the Samuel Jackson character in *A Time to Kill*) who should probably be free. They are almost always arrogant, often venal, generally incompetent, and, with few exceptions, little more than foils for heroic cops or crusading defense attorneys.

Reality, of course, is never so simple. As one prosecutor lamented, "The public never sees us holding the victim's hand, which is ninety percent of what we do." Prosecutors, no less than defense attorneys, come at all levels of compassion, commitment, and competence. Yet unlike so many attorneys in private practice, few do it primarily for the money. The job simply does not pay enough in most jurisdictions to elevate one above the status of the lower middle class. Some, of course, take the job merely to punch a ticket (and gain trial experience) en route to a lucrative career in corporate litigation or in defending, for enormous fees, the very types they previously put in jail. Others, however, do it at substantial economic sacrifice because they believe in the mission of being advocates "for the people" or in the virtue of standing up for the rights of the victimized or because they can't abide the idea of crossing over to the other side and working to obtain the freedom of those who destroy lives without remorse.

Dilulio, of course, applauds prosecutors for performing a valuable public service. And in "White Lies about Black Crime," published in the Winter 1995 issue of the *Public Interest*, he compared the plight of black people to that of the Italians in an earlier era:

> Not too many decades ago, members of that part of my Italian-American family who hail from West Virginia were segregated from "whites" in public schools. Other parts of the family from the East Coast to the Midwest also suffered various forms of discrimination. Some overcame; most worked hard; a few lived the American dream.
>
> Yet, no matter what they achieved, they labored under the disgraceful reality of the Mafia. Italians killing Italians. Italians murdering, extorting, corrupting, and thereby creating a self-defaming cultural image which, even to this day, no Italian in any walk of life can ever fully escape. Should I, then, as an Italian-American, feel the least bit "ambivalent" when a big-city Italian prosecutor puts away a bunch of Italian-American criminals for life? Does the society need any

special Italian-American "authorization" to lock these people up or put them on death row? No way.

The very fact that Dilulio could even talk about "black crime," however, is evidence that the way America regards blacks and the way it regarded Italians is not precisely the same. After all, Dilulio did not talk of "Italian crime," but of crime committed by the Mafia. In other words, he did not characterize crime itself with the adjective "Italian," even when he acknowledged that Italians were disproportionately involved in some spectacularly ugly misdeeds. Yet, as Andrew Hacker noted in the *Nation*, "Crime has been given a racial coloration. Indeed, 'black crime' is regarded as different and more fearsome than other forms of lawbreaking. . . . Why the racial appellation? Of course, white people commit felonies, among them terrorizing clinics, blowing up a daycare center and devising savings and loan swindles and Fortune 500 frauds. (Interestingly, the latter are called 'white-collar crime,' not 'white crime,' even when all the perpetrators are Caucasian.)" Hacker's point is that black Americans are under siege in society in general, not only by black criminals, and that in the context of that larger war, it is necessary to consider the ubiquitous role that racism and the fears of whites play. To pretend that the way we view—and treat—criminals has nothing to do with their race is, as Hacker sees it, to be in a self-delusional state.

Hacker noted that each semester he presents his white students at Queens College with the hypothetical choice of being robbed of $100 by someone who is black or of $300 by someone who is white. Virtually all choose the white robber. As he explained:

> It is not simply that they feel blacks are more drawn to violence. Far more at issue is the fear that the man in front of them will take another moment and do something horrible, to repay the white race for what it has done to his people. So "black crime" is not mainly about taking money or articles of value, or even about demands at gunpoint. For white Americans, it represents racial revenge, as if each robbery—or rape—is part of an ongoing insurrection. It is the same fear slaveowners had of being slaughtered in their beds. And compounding the dread is the sense that the man facing you has nothing to lose, that he has been in prison before, and the prospect of returning there does not frighten him.

Hence, whites are all too eager to lock up the black threat, even if they know that it costs more to send a young man to jail than to send him to Harvard, for many, if not most, whites regard jail as "a safer investment."

Dilulio, of course, dismisses such notions as irrelevant and such language as demagogic. Do racist laws, he asked, explain why the rates of arrests for carrying weapons are five times greater for blacks than for whites? "Do they explain the fact that 47 percent of all black men in prison in 1995 were in for a *violent crime*, and that most black state prisoners, like most state prisoners, have committed one or more violent crimes in the past?" And even if, for argument's sake, one accepts the notion that blacks are disproportionately punished by current law, what then? Should we just let black lawbreakers go free? "Which drug-crime 911 calls from black neighborhoods are the police to ignore? Which black drug dealers should be released back to their communities tomorrow morning?"

The question, as Dilulio is well aware, has no easy answer, and perhaps no answer at all as long as the problem is viewed within the narrow context of the criminal justice system. Rather, the problems of crime in black communities (as distinguished from the ridiculous locution "black crime") and of arrest rates of black citizens ultimately encompass issues that are much larger than those handled by the criminal courts. The justice system is, in many respects, the last stop on the road. It is a dumping ground for people whom life has failed and who, in turn, have failed at life. Dealing honestly and intelligently with the problem of black convicts means focusing, in a way that this nation is loath to do, on the myriad conditions—of miseducation, misdirection, and missing opportunities—that create so many of them. To castigate black prosecutors for society's failure to make black criminals into productive citizens, however, is a bit like castigating the man who tries his best to defend his home and his family against those who are intent on doing them harm. The man under siege can deal only with the problem on his doorstep, and at that point his options are lamentably and severely limited. He can resist or he can step aside and try not to reflect on the heartbreak that will surely follow. Defense lawyers have no greater range of options, for they, too, are dealing with the consequences of society's failure. On the one hand, if they are sufficiently gifted, they can hide that fact under a symbolic cloud and harness the well-founded mistrust of judicial integrity in black communities on behalf of their own agenda. On the other hand, if they are being truthful, they will acknowledge that they don't have the answers either and that they are certainly no more heroic or even representative than the so-called Uncle Toms they may, in the pursuit of victory, denounce. At best, they are trying to make a bad system work slightly better; at worst, they are pimping on their own behalf as they sell "wolf tickets" to distract those (such as Darden during the Simpson trial) who attempt to hold them and their clients accountable.

In *The Fire Next Time*, James Baldwin asked: "Do I really *want* to be integrated into a burning house?" Many black (and Latino) prosecutors in America find themselves pondering a variation on that question: "Do I really *want* to remain in a justice system that has become a funeral pyre for so many African American (and Latino) dreams?" Some, like Darden, seem disinclined to stay; the long-term psychological cost just seems too high a price to pay. Yet others are determined to soldier on. In the same way that Baldwin saw blacks as the potential saviors of America, they see themselves as perhaps the system's only and best hope—and certainly the best hope of the men and women of color who are forced, either by their own actions or the actions of others, to seek justice in America's courts. Still, they know that to stay in that system is to accept the possibility that, in the end, they may be fatally burned.

Ellis Cose *is the editor of this volume and a contributing editor to* Newsweek. *Former chairman of the editorial board and editorial page editor of the* New York Daily News, *he began his journalism career at age nineteen as a columnist for the* Chicago Sun-Times. *Cose has been a contributor to, and press critic of,* Time *magazine, chief writer on management and workplace issues for* USA Today, *and member of the editorial board of the* Detroit Free Press. *He is also the author of several books, including* The Rage of a Privileged Class, A Man's World, *and* Color-Blind.

Reasonable Doubt
MARCIA ANN GILLESPIE

Where to begin? For me, an African American woman who was born as World War II was coming to its bloody conclusion, discussions of race and justice in this society invariably conjure up memories of a time that many people in this country would like to forget. My memories, and those of my generation, blend with those of my parents and their parents' age mates that I grew up hearing told and retold, but they bear little resemblance to what Bob Dole rhapsodizes about when he talks about a kinder, gentler bygone era. Those difficult memories that I share with generations of African Americans would no longer seem relevant if they didn't continue to be reenacted in our society, often in subtler but no less lethal forms; if they didn't continue to shape and inform my response to the issues and events that swirl around me; if racism was not still a clear and present danger. So I begin with my memories and the questions they sparked.

When I was a kid growing up on Long Island during the 1950s, I used to wonder if white people ever had the police come rampaging through their neighborhoods, if they got their heads cracked open with billy clubs, if they were they dumped in police cars like sacks of potatoes and thrown in jail willy-nilly on a hot Saturday night. Oh yes, I'd seen the occasional headlines and plenty of old movies in which guys called Lefty or Big Al were sent up to the Big House, so I knew that white gangsters, notorious murderers, and people who were found guilty of treason, like the Rosenbergs, were locked away in places like Sing-Sing prison waiting to be executed. But I also knew what I saw on a regular basis in my neighborhood and all too often on the pages of the local newspapers—black men being carted off to jail.

Forty years ago, practically the only time when black people who were not entertainers or sports figures got mentioned in mainstream newspapers was when they were charged with or found guilty of a crime. My white elementary school classmates, who lived in seemingly quiet neighborhoods, never seemed to have stories to tell about watching cops wielding truncheons like berserkers. It was as if only black people played and ran the numbers; got drunk; cursed; and fought with fists, bottles, and knives, as if only black men beat their wives and girlfriends, as if we were the only folks who broke the law, only us, always us, all of us.

Did those classmates of mine ever have cause to question or doubt our system of justice and the people who were hired to enforce it? Were stories told around their kitchen tables of the indignities suffered at the hands of the police, of people routinely insulted or threatened, of men being beaten for no reason, or of false arrests, coerced confessions, and sham trials? Was the name Emmett Till indelibly imprinted in their memories? Did stark images of "strange fruit" hanging from Southern trees disrupt their sleep?

Once their breasts started budding, did the girls quickly learn to beware our local policemen, to walk briskly when patrol cars cruised slowly alongside them and pretend not to hear or see those men in blue as they hissed and cajoled them to climb in the car and have a "good time"? Were the boys routinely followed and questioned when they ventured outside their neighborhoods? And what of their parents, who, though no more respectable, honest, and hardworking than mine, were routinely treated with deference and respect by the same white policemen who rarely (as in almost never) bothered to address a black adult as Mr., Mrs., or Miss? Were they even aware of what happened on the colored side of town? When they read in the newspapers about yet another black person being arrested, charged, or convicted, did they pause to question what they were reading? Did they discuss the impact of poor housing, poverty, racism, police brutality, and a color-charged justice system? Perhaps some of them did, but more than likely, even the most sympathetic shook their heads in a mixture of disgust and bewilderment and said things like, "That's just the way so many of them are."

Do I overstate the situation? Given that white social thinkers across the political spectrum usually characterized issues of race in the United States as the Negro Problem, I don't think so. The stereotypes and myths that had been used to justify slavery and the U.S. apartheid system were very much intact. The notion of the lazy, venal, good-for-nothing, hot-blooded, over-sexed, violent, childlike, morally loose, criminally inclined Negro was powerfully appealing to white America. And historically, the justice system helped to reinforce this belief. According to popular lore, we were either good and faithful God-fearing subservients; playful, fun-loving, natural-born entertainers; or "jungle-bunnies" with voracious sexual appetites, animal cunning, and feral instincts. Uncle Tom and Porgy and Beulah or Bess and Stagger Lee. Always there were the lingering questions. Did Uncle Tom have a heart of darkness; could he be a Bigger Thomas? On Saturday night, did Mammy put on her red petticoat and turn into Carmen Jones? Were all blacks criminally inclined; was it just our nature?

Even people who were willing to believe that justice for black Americans was hard if not impossible to come by south of the Mason-Dixon line were often seduced into believing that we were more often guilty than innocent. Or else they were quick to attribute the problem to the South's racism. But most whites who lived outside Dixie were equally committed to the carefully cultivated fiction that the justice system in their states, cities, towns, and villages was untainted. Clinging to the comfortable notion that racism was a Southern redneck thing created a moral comfort zone. Whenever charges of police harassment and brutality, false arrests, coerced confessions, railroading, biased judges and juries, harsher sentencing, and wrongful imprisonments and executions were raised, the predictable response was shocked disbelief. Far too few seemed willing to recognize that our system of justice was almost schizophrenic in its response to and treatment of black people—on the one hand, overzealous in its use of force, but on the other hand, relatively indifferent to the routine violations of our civil rights.

"I know, I know," I can hear some people saying, "that was then, this is now; things have changed. We have sung 'We Shall Overcome,' and the apartheid system has been dismantled; look at the progress so many of your people have made. There are black police, police chiefs, district attorneys, judges, mayors, and members of Congress. Look at Jesse Jackson, Colin Powell, and all those millionaires who don't sing, dance, act, or play ball, plus all the ones who do. Look at the booming middle class living in their suburban enclaves, driving their high-priced foreign cars, and sending their kids to Ivy League schools. It's a new day."

In this "new day" of techno-speak and virtual reality, we are asked to believe that race—that is, racism—is no longer the issue. The United States no longer has a "Negro problem"; class is the conundrum, specifically the underclass. That the perpetrators and usual suspects who appear with deadening regularity on local television news broadcasts and real-life cop shows are most frequently black and Latino is not a racial thing; it's just because "they happen to be part of the underclass." But is it mere happenstance that "they"—the wild, unkempt, disheveled men and women; the teenagers in their hip-hop gear; and the welfare cheats, gang bangers, drug dealers, prostitutes, muggers, murderers, and rapists paraded across our local news reports—are usually people of color?

Do African Americans commit more crimes? If you look at who is in prison, the answer would seem fairly simple. In 1994, the year O. J. Simpson was charged with the murders of his former wife, Nicole Brown Simpson, and Ronald Goldman, for every one white man who was incarcerated, there were eight black men, and for every white woman, there were seven black women. In 1995, the year O. J. was found not guilty, on any given day, one in three black men in their twenties were either in prison or jail or on probation or parole, as were 5 percent of all black women in the same age group. But as study after study has shown, America's so-called War on Drugs, which is propped up with smoke and mirrors and lots of arrests of folks who are more the victims than the victimizers, has a great deal to do with those statistics. Possessing a vial of crack, the drug of poverty, will land you in jail a whole lot quicker than possessing an ounce of cocaine, the middle-class drug of choice. Given that blacks are most often shown being arrested for possessing drugs, images that constantly reinforce the stereotype of the bad "nigger," it's easy to believe that we are the major users. The fact that drug use by blacks is not higher than that by whites—just our arrest rates—gets lost in the shuffle. Are the laws race based? Is the justice system color blind or color coded? Have the times really changed?

Do I sound cynical? Given what I know, what my eyes have seen, the all-too-familiar stories that abound, and what I myself have experienced of this system, a certain degree of skepticism is the only healthy response.

The notorious "N" word—and all that it implies—which caused such heat in the courtroom during the Simpson trial, floats just beneath the surface. It fuels so much of the outrage about welfare, the pontificating about family values, and the increasing hostility toward the "undeserving" poor. The images of Stagger Lee and Bad Beulah helped spark the resurrection of the Southern chain gang, the cry for the criminalization of pregnant women who are drug addicted, for more prisons, "three strikes and you're out," and the death penalty. That most of the people who are sitting on death row are brown and beige or that the death penalty is most often invoked in cases in which blacks are charged with killing whites and the defendants are poor isn't just a fluke. Yes, in almost every society, the poor are the ones who are the most exposed to crime as both perpetrators and victims, are most likely to run afoul of the justice system, and are its most frequent pawns. But in the United States, race and poverty are so inextricably bound that the reactionary response of containing "them" is often played out in terms of keeping the dangerous, despised, colored others at bay.

But being a bona fide member of the middle or upper class is no protection. All across this country, young African Americans, no matter their socioeconomic class, are routinely stopped by the police and questioned for little or no reason, save for the fact that their age, and especially the color of their skin, makes them automatically suspect. Ask any black mother of a teenage son, whether she lives in the heart of the ghetto or in a gated suburban enclave, what her biggest fear for her child is, and invariably she will speak about him running afoul of the law and being harassed, beaten, falsely arrested, or shot. Our children are considered suspicious because of the clothes they wear and the color of their skin, because of the music they play and the color of their skin, because of the cars they drive and the color of their skin, because they hang out in malls and the color of their skin. Or simply because of the color of their skin, as was the case when a young business-suited magazine executive who was commuting by train from his suburban New York home was roughed up and arrested by the transit police because he supposedly looked like a suspect. It did not matter that he bore no resemblance to the wanted man except for the fact that they were both black. The incident, which was like so many others as to seem almost mundane, took on a higher profile only because the man's father, a prominent, politically well-connected magazine owner, raised a ruckus.

Shall I also tell you of the time I was thrown out of a Manhattan police station in the middle of the night because I dared to reprimand the desk sergeant who had insulted me? Or of all the stories turned into bittersweet jokes that I've heard friends and associates tell of their close encounters of the cop kind: the stops and searches for no reason, the use of excessive force, the disregard of our complaints?

Forty years and thousands of charges later, it took a videotape of Rodney King being beaten again and again into the ground to "validate," in the eyes of most of white America, what we've been saying all along. And once again we hear the same refrain—the expressions of shock and surprise and outrage, followed by the quick disclaimers: "It was an isolated incident" or "It could never happen here." And meanwhile, court dockets and jails and prisons continue to fill with beige- and brown-skinned people. A voracious, rampaging river of drugs floods our poorest communities, where housing and education deteriorate; unemployment and under-employment run rampant; and broken families, self-destructive behavior, violent crime, fear, and hopeless-ness corrode the spirit and ensure the continued growth of the new penal plantations. While we talk about black genocide, the need for self-help, personal and commu-nal responsibility and empowerment, factories close, family farms disappear, the job pool for manual laborers shrinks, and members of the working class are recycled as employees of the prison industry. And still most of white America continues to cling to the notion that racism is nothing more than a series of regrettable but isolated incidents that African Americans tend to blow all out of proportion.

In a patriarchal society, racial justice invariably becomes an issue of manhood. The treacherous ways that the justice system has been used to oppress black men is one of the earliest civics lessons we learn. It is no wonder, then, that the term *reasonable doubt* takes on a much greater significance to many of us when Stagger Lee's on trial. It's difficult not to question police reports, the evidence, and even eyewitness accounts when the witnesses are white, knowing as we do how rarely they seem to note that we all don't look alike, or to trust the judge or the prosecutors automatically. Reasonable doubt has a history attached to it and a color. For many of the people who cheered O. J. Simpson's acquittal, the role of an admittedly racist cop in gathering the evidence was cause for reasonable doubt. They cheered because a black man, Johnnie Cochran, defending a black man, O. J. Simpson, beat a system we've come to distrust.

Let us not forget that we are not the only people in this society who distrust the system or sometimes root for the "bad" guy. Time and again, we've seen law-abiding citizens respond to desperadoes more as if they were celebrities than villains. People who are scrambling to make ends meet applaud the bank robber who parachutes out of a plane with millions of dollars. While we cry for law and order, we also complain about the loss of our personal freedoms and resent the government's intrusiveness. So we vilify and romanticize the Mafia, flock to see films in which the characters we root for routinely break the law, and call for more prisons. Most of us are somewhat skeptical of the system, believing it plays favorites and that money and having the right connections make a world of difference.

Is there a dilemma here? Only for those who fail to recognize that racism continues to have an impact on everyone in this society—it's simply a matter of degree—coloring our perceptions and creating Rashomon-like versions of reality. As long as the Stagger Lee and Bad Beulah stereotypes keep being replayed and as long as racism is played out in classrooms and corporations, in employment and housing, in social policies and political debates, and in the mass media, it will be a factor in the courtroom.

As much as this angers me, I am equally outraged by

the fact that as long as issues of race are defined by patriarchy, black women remain mere handmaids to the larger male agenda. As was true a hundred years ago, today, what's good for the race is defined by patriarchy as what's good for black men and by what black men define the issues to be. At the dawn of this century, to be called a "race woman" was one of the highest compliments a black woman could be paid. It meant that you worked tirelessly on behalf of your people. Race women were usually clubwomen and churchwomen whose good works rarely strayed beyond the confines of what were considered properly ladylike activities: patriarchal, acceptable race work. Today, the terms *good black woman* or *righteous sister* are usually employed in much the same way, as compliments extended to women whose activities conform to the patriarchy's agenda and seen as supportive of black people in general. Racism as it affects women, in particular, has always been considered secondary, and the discussion of sexism is often viewed with suspicion and hostility or as an act of disloyalty.

This situation further explains why so little emphasis is placed on the huge increase in the number of black women in prison and why this society's response to women's victimization by men is often racially charged. Patriarchy on all sides of the racial divide has instilled a particular loathing for women who run afoul of the law. Thus, even though black women are the fastest-growing group in the prison population, men remain the focus of our concern, rage, and political action. Since female drug addicts get little sympathy and less help, the move to criminalize pregnant drug addicts is met with relatively little resistance. The pregnant drug addict is considered an unnatural woman, better locked up than treated. The woman who strikes back at her abusive mate becomes a danger to society, better locked up after the fact than adequately protected beforehand.

The questions that spur reasonable doubt, that almost automatically come into play when Stagger Lee is on trial, are often overshadowed by certain sexist assumptions about women's roles and place, about those considered Bad Beulahs. When black women run afoul of the law, either as victims or as suspected criminals, all the worst racial and sexual stereotypes come raging to the fore. Because black women are considered more aggressive than their white sisters, the police feel justified in using greater force to subdue them. Because aggressive women are universally suspect, the black community tends to back away. Because black women are considered sexually loose, charges of rape, especially if the alleged attacker or attackers are also black, are less likely to be believed by a jury. The young black woman who dared charge Mike Tyson with rape became an object of scorn among many in the black community for bringing a successful brother down. But the young black woman who falsely cried rape by a group of whites became a heroine, and her case became a cause célèbre for many blacks. So Anita Hill became a reluctant witness and was vilified by many for publicly claiming that Clarence Thomas harassed her. But despite all the questions and challenges raised about his caring for or allegiance to African Americans, Thomas knew exactly the right buttons to push when he denounced those Senate hearings as a "high-tech lynching."

It's all part of the paradox that racism has created in this society. We obey the laws, pay our taxes, join the police force, go to law school, wear the black robes, and distrust the system. We call for greater black representation in the judicial system, hoping that these representatives of ours will bring our memories, our skepticism, and a real determination to eliminate, or at least help mitigate, the racism in the system. And we want them to be racially aware, while we pray that they will not be seduced into believing that their mere presence indicates that the system works. It shouldn't take a jury acquittal to make a black district attorney face the fact that not only is an admittedly racist cop a detriment to the case if the defendant is black, but that he or she symbolizes all we have come to loathe and fear about the system. Christopher Darden and Marcia Clark lost their case against O. J. Simpson the moment they chose not to believe that race is always a factor. They chose to be among the 'shocked' and 'surprised.' So instead of responding, they reacted—Darden by playing out the patriarchy's game of race as a "manhood" thing, trading verbal punches, and Clark, by assuming that African

American women would automatically place a woman's issue above race. And we witnessed what comes of that kind of arrogance and ignorance in the courtroom.

Yes, we want law and order in our communities, but we also harbor a deep distrust of the police and the court system. Yes, we bring to the witness stand and the jury box our memories of and experiences with the law, our understanding of the subtle and not-so-subtle ways that racism plays out in our lives, our awareness of the stereotypes that continue to shape how others perceive us, as we rightly should. (Just as all people bring the baggage of their histories and experiences, their prejudices and hopes, to the process.) Yes, we have good reason to doubt. Yes, as long as race is prioritized and defined along patriarchal lines, issues of justice for black women will remain sidelined. Yes, we resent and despair of the fact that this society seems determined to avoid any sustained discussion of our continuing racial divide, preferring instead to be "shocked" and "surprised" by those incidents that cannot be easily swept under the national rug, while denying that racism is still deeply entrenched. Yet somehow, despite all the baggage we carry, all the freight of race in America, our belief in justice still resonates. And it is that belief that has helped keep this society from being torn asunder.

How many videotapes must be shown before our memories, our realities, our experiences, our sensibilities, our skepticism, and our reasonable doubts, as well as our often sorely tried faith in the possibility of justice, are acknowledged, respected, and addressed? I'd like to lay my memories to rest.

Marcia Ann Gillespie is the editor-in-chief and former executive editor of Ms. magazine. Before she joined Ms., she was an editorial consultant for such magazines and organizations as Life magazine, the Children's Defense Fund, and the University of the West Indies. During her tenure as editor-in-chief of Essence, the magazine won the National Magazine Award, and Gillespie was named one of the Fifty Faces for America's Future by Time magazine. She has written extensively on issues of gender and race.

The Precarious Balance:
Race Man or Sellout?
Elijah Anderson

During the course of the O. J. Simpson trial, Christopher Darden became a popular target for accusations of selling out. Why he was so charged is complicated by the fact that many of those who share that opinion of Darden also realize that O. J. is probably guilty, even though his guilt wasn't proved beyond a reasonable doubt. Still, however, many find themselves disgusted with a black man who would prosecute another.

The divisive racial atmosphere in which we live makes such a seemingly contradictory stance understandable. We now have an increasingly diverse black middle class in the midst of a black working class that has seen its fortunes decline rapidly with the industry that supported it. In turn, the weakest members of the working class find themselves slipping into the growing underclass. The Republican Right stirs up the latent racism of those who are inclined to see black people as incompetent, at best, and, at worst, freeloaders who are getting something for nothing. At the same time, black leaders, such as Louis Farrakhan, fan the flames of separatism, challenging whether whites are really worthy of integration. From this larger lens, we then narrow the focus to Simpson and the two white people who were brutally murdered, and to Darden, who was working for the prosecution (and who, some people say, was used as a token black to legitimate the case against a prominent black).

Ironically, before the moment when Darden and Simpson entered the courtroom from opposite sides, most would have seen the diligent Darden as the race man and Simpson, the millionaire amateur golfer and widely esteemed ex–football great, television salesman, and sports announcer, as the sellout. But as soon as the trial began, Darden's and Simpson's positions appear to have been reversed. What happened?

The dilemma experienced by Darden when he agreed to prosecute another black man is perhaps a dilemma that many blacks in professional positions are experiencing to an increasing degree. So many of these blacks face the dual pressures and expectations of being "professionals" in a white world and of dealing with what it means to be African American in the 1990s. The choice of coming to terms with their situations as blacks or as professionals, as the example of Darden shows, is not always left up to them. This coming to terms is made all the more painful by those who see racial loyalty as an either/or proposition—you're either for us or against us, a race man or a sellout.

The idea of the race man goes back to the segregated black community, in fact, all the way back to the time of slavery. The term itself comes from the classic ethnographic study of the black community in Chicago, *Black Metropolis*, carried out in the 1940s by two sociologists at the University of Chicago, Horace Cayton and St. Clair Drake. By Cayton and Drake's definition, the race man (or woman) was a particular kind of black leader who lived in a segregated society and felt strongly responsible to the black race, especially in front of whites or outsiders to the community. Often, he felt as though he carried the whole weight of the race on his shoulders, and in public had the need to put matters of race first. Such a person was intent on "advancing the race" by working as a role model, both to uplift the ghetto community and to disabuse the wider society of its often negative view of blacks.

In this effort to advance the race against American apartheid, every other black was looked on as a natural ally—a brother, a cousin, or a friend. Everyone who was "somebody," not just professionals and politicians, but hardworking industrial union members, the "regulars" on the corner, and the neighborhood "grandmothers," wanted to be and were bound to be race men and

women. Implicit in this belief was a kind of racial solidarity, a peculiar celebration of racial "particularism," of
putting matters of race above all other issues. There
were community secrets that blacks shared among
themselves and perhaps with white "friends of the
race," but in the face of the general white community,
black people expected to close their ranks and be silent.
And for a long time, there was a critical mass of race
men and women in the black community.

The birth of the race man came at a time when there
was a caste-like system in the culture as a whole and a
particularly rigid wall of segregation between blacks
and whites in terms of styles of life, behavior, culture,
residence, and power. The race man flourished in that
caste-like system. White people, not grasping the full
significance of the role, often called such a person a
"credit to his race." At the impetus of the civil rights
movement and the insurgencies and civil disorders of
the 1960s, the white system started the process of
granting blacks civil rights and incorporating blacks
more fully into the economic system. By the 1970s, a
black middle class was developing, increasingly assimilated with the white system. But one of the costs of
becoming a trusted member of this system is to divest
oneself, to some extent, of one's own ethnic particular-
ity and to display a commitment to the values of the
dominant culture. Adopting this posture works against
the ideology of the race man; the more his people are
assimilated, the less important is his role. Thus, the

process we've been witnessing on a large scale in the past quarter century is the emergence of a new type of black professional who, even though he or she often experiences divided loyalties, appears as interested in his or her class or profession as in his or her race.

This process is, in many respects, similar to what the Irish, Jews, Italians, and other ethnic groups have undergone. All these groups have had their race men at certain times in their histories, but as the groups' fortunes have risen, the need for their respective race men has declined and other individuals have emerged who are increasingly more interested in their professions and class positions. These individuals don't necessarily forget their roots, but often the needs of their profession win out, and class issues take precedence over public displays of ethnic and racial particularism. This is what we have come to expect as a normal consequence of upward mobility in the United States. The exception is that of race and the nature and complexity of racism that blacks face. In particular, this is the system in which people like Darden came of age.

Since the civil rights movement, when Darden was just a child, many individuals have become absorbed by the system. They were educated, applied themselves, and were offered professional positions within the establishment. As a result, they became upwardly mobile and were able to get in on the American Dream, while striving for the full rights, obligations, and privileges of upper-middle-class Americans. All in all, they willingly separated themselves from the mass of blacks. In such settings, they experienced a new type of segregation, largely of their own making. For the inner city, they were still role models, but they were increasingly role models from a distance—a distance that has mattered to blacks in a way that is vastly different from the way it mattered to other ethnic groups in the past.

In the 1990s, after this age of integration and the gradual loss of traditional race men and women, we have seen the emergence of Farrakhan, the Rodney King beating and its aftermath, the Simpson case, the Million Man March, and the implicit marginalization of people like Jesse Jackson, Coretta Scott King, and moderate black leaders who actively supported integration. It is a period in which someone like Farrakhan preaches separatism to ambivalent, if not receptive audiences. A concomitant, parallel development has been the emergence of an oppositional culture among black youths, especially in the inner cities. Unlike many of their parents and grandparents, these young people often pride themselves on being racially particularistic and on buying into ideas, norms, and notions of society that are often diametrically opposed to "white" conventions, the norms of the wider society. And this attitude appears to be spreading; fueled by an increasingly resistant white system, it is one of the most dramatic developments in the black community today.

In the United States of the 1990s, at a time of heightened feelings by blacks of being persecuted by the society at large, the race man has reemerged to defend and serve the group. But this time it is a new race man. The former race men were integrationists, striving to attain the same rights, duties, and privileges for blacks that were claimed by whites. In contrast, Farrakhan and others like him are promoting separatism. Their goals for the black society—such as self-reliance and stable families—are largely shared by the white society, but they see the ideal black society as parallel to, rather than an integrated part of, the white society. Several factors have been at work to bring this situation about, some obvious and well documented and some perhaps more subtle.

One element is the growing trend toward ethnicity and particularism among groups throughout the wider society (and the world), including some of the newer waves of immigrants. Many of these recent immigrants are educated people, not poor or working-class people, so they are under less pressure than previous immigrants to divest themselves of their ethnic identities in exchange for upward mobility. They are encouraged to hold on to their particularities and even to celebrate them as cultural diversity, and groups from previous waves are joining in that trend. Blacks, having always been apart from the wider society to a large extent, have a real and justified interest in buying into their own ethnicity, celebrating it, becoming ethnocentric. And many do.

Strongly related to these considerations are the many

forces that are pressing on the inner-city black population today. Repeatedly, blacks have witnessed the precipitous rise and fall in their fortunes through slavery, emancipation, segregation, the civil rights movement, affirmative action, and now political retrenchment as politicians are gaining political clout by proving themselves hostile to the advancement of blacks. Today, we are experiencing the transformation of American cities from centers of manufacturing to centers of service and high technology. The loss of well-paying manufacturing jobs in the cities as U.S. corporations have sent their low-skill jobs to Third World countries and nonmetropolitan areas of this country has devastated the black working class. The resulting poverty has created a social breakdown in our inner cities on a huge scale—witness the all-too-familiar and escalating problems of alienation, drug abuse, violence, teenage pregnancy, family disintegration, record rates of arrest and incarceration, AIDS, homelessness, and endemic joblessness.

At the heart of the matter, and of the rise in the fortunes of this new generation of more separatist race men, is the dominant culture's denigration of the character and competence of black men. Because men are considered to be responsible for providing for the welfare of their families and communities in our society, many people who are confronted with the widespread unemployment of black people have reached a simple conclusion: There is something terribly wrong with the black man. His moral fiber, his common decency, his very masculinity are being called into question. In any discussion of prisons, welfare, joblessness, family desertion, crime, violence, or drugs, his name is invoked. Shopkeepers fear him. Taxi drivers refuse to pick him up. It has become easy to grumble that he is the reason for our nation's problems. And some politicians have responded by slashing welfare and ignoring economic and structural realities, such as the aforementioned devastation of the inner cities, threatening to turn back a generation of racial gains.

We now know that one in three black men aged twenty to thirty is in the hands of the criminal justice system—in jail, on probation, or awaiting adjudication. The reasons for this high rate of involvement in the criminal justice system are at least twofold. As the situation of the impoverished inner-city black man has become increasingly untenable, he has been left without the resources to sustain a family. We have thus witnessed an enormous increase in female-headed households and the increasing feminization of poverty. Children grow up in these households without adequate resources, but also without the support of role models who can help them grow up to be productive, law-abiding citizens. Indeed, in the most distressed families, the purveyors of popular culture become the role models for children who are then left to bridge for themselves the gap between what they are shown their lives should be like and what their daily reality is.

But although poverty and the desperation it breeds in

these communities are certainly at least partly at fault for such a shocking statistic, no less a contributing factor is the severe scrutiny that the criminal justice system inflicts on people who are identified as belonging to these self-destructing communities. Outside these communities, in particular, such people are too often penalized for things that other people may not even be noticed for. Yet, in these distressed areas, they continue to try to come to terms with their world, to seek to be whole in light of so much misery and destitution; that, to say the least, is a challenge. The life of a young inner-city black person is all but guaranteed to be deeply alienating.

All this has grave implications for young blacks. To be a worthwhile person, the cultural apparatus of the mass media preaches, is to aspire to materialism. In lieu of an education and a good job, a certain amount of form and display and conspicuous consumption proclaims "I'm a good person, too." And nobody wants to make this claim more strongly than do young black people who are caught in these compromised situations. So they are encouraged to do whatever it takes to realize themselves through materialism and to obtain material things. For young inner-city blacks, however, there are few legitimate opportunities to obtain the money to satisfy such desires. And when the regular economy fails to respond, the stage is set for the emergence and elaboration of the irregular or "underground" economy, which expands and thus creates its own problems. As some young blacks obtain material treasures through these illicit means, they can become utterly confused, in the racist public mind, with those who obtain the same material things through legitimate means.

Many middle-class youths, black as well as white, often revel in such confusion to an extent, attempting to give the signal that they are "from the ghetto" and gaining status points for being "rough," "mean," or "bad." But many other youths who are members of the growing black middle class work just as hard to draw distinctions between themselves and the youths of the inner city. If some of these people embrace the image of the tough inner-city youth, there are many others who don't look back and certainly don't reach back, fervently believing that their fortunes lie in placing the widest possible distance between themselves and such inner-city youths. It may be politically correct to pretend to reach back, but many of these young people, as well as their parents, want no part of the inner-city experience. And those who do want to reach back often simply do not know how.

Implicit here is the profound realization that in American society, simply being black poses a special problem of social, psychological, or even physical survival. In the black community, the idea has arisen that black people pay a special tax just to get along day to day. Since the Rodney King beating, in particular, middle-class blacks, working-class blacks, and poor blacks often, and perhaps increasingly, agree on this point. As a young black man once told me, "When you get stopped by a policeman on the road and are given a ticket, you accept it, but at the same time you wonder whether he stopped you because you are black. When you see another black man stopped by the police, you wonder how race figured into it. When you go into a store and the salespeople give you an extra bit of scrutiny, you wonder. When you're on the elevator in your apartment building and the elevator stops at a floor and the white woman waiting moves over to another elevator, your first thought is race. Little things like that remind you as a black person that you are paying your black tax." Occasionally, more flagrant incidents occur, especially when the people who do the insulting think they can be anonymous. Many college campuses provide ample opportunities for those who are intent on exacting the black tax. Black students report being called "nigger," having urine-filled balloons thrown at them, or being subjected to hostile shouts from windows of dormitories. One black professor told me that he had eggs thrown at him from a dormitory window. Of course, relatively few white students are engaging in this kind of behavior, but enough are doing so to exacerbate black people's feeling of being under fire by the larger society.

Meanwhile, in public interactions, blacks' images of themselves may be called into question by the set of negative stereotypes that emerge from the mass media's reports on the plight of the underclass. Although one could argue that the criminal activities of the black man are unavoidably newsworthy, at the same time they send a message of extreme black pathology, thereby creating a severe public relations problem. While the racially enlightened citizenry may be able to contextualize, make distinctions, and individualize these problems, this is not always the case for those who lack knowledge of the history of race relations in this country and a sophisticated understanding of individual circumstances. A segment of the white population seems to have embraced the most negative image of the black man that results from the reportage, and many of them go to the polls with this generalized stereotype and vote for policies that make things worse.

And it is not just working-class whites who often lack the ability to make distinctions. The confusion occurs among the highly educated as well, black and white alike. What such confused persons fail to grasp is that the problems of the black underclass are rooted in the structural changes that have gutted the availability of lower-skill jobs. And without job opportunities, new cultural adaptations and survival strategies have been developed that often complicate the initial problem profoundly. Tragically, many of the wider citizenry, who, in the expanding economy of the "civil rights" era once supported social programs to alleviate the conditions undermining so much of ghetto life, have now apparently turned against blacks and the social policies that made their advancement possible in the first place.

The young inner-city black man has not failed to respond to this state of affairs. Often resigned to a society that does not include him in the American Dream, he comes of age realizing the hard truths that American society is not there for him, that a racially stratified system is in place, and that his place, fortified through acts of prejudice and discrimination, is at the bottom of it. This creates in him a profound sense of alienation and forces him to adapt, to make some adjustments. That resignation can be observed in the young men's looks, in their actions, and in their tendency to disparage white people except for those who can be used to attain a goal. Life has taught the young black man that he can do certain things but cannot go beyond his limited situation; dreams are simply never fulfilled. He knows the dream that says people will "judge you not by the color of your skin, but by the content of your character," but he also knows "the real deal"—that he must always pay a tax for being black in America. A common response is to embrace the profound alienation represented by the oppositional culture of the street.

Even the black men who win—"make it" in mainstream society—must have a certain distrust of the prize: Their own success alienates them from the black masses but fails to win them true acceptance by the wider system. Those young middle-class black men who acquire the resources to negotiate the wider system and who, in the process, have worked so hard to eliminate any potential confusion between them and their inner-city counterparts feel eternally in limbo between two extremes: the drug-dealing, gold-wearing street hustler who "disses" the conventions of the wider society, on the one hand, and the successful mainstream professional, on the other hand. Therefore, black professionals must constantly struggle to define themselves on their own terms, in the context of a society that both demonizes and celebrates them (O. J. Simpson being a good case in point). All this contributes to a certain precariousness of place that results from people's presuppositions with regard to the black man. The black man's color and maleness become his master status, putting into question anything else he may claim to be.

Darden's dilemma, therefore, is one he shares with many African Americans. He was trying to serve two basically contradictory gods, that of black racial particularism and that of meritocracy and universalism. His attempt to serve either one at any given time could easily be interpreted as a betrayal by followers of the other. To be seen as fair in terms of the merits of the case, he had to bend over backwards to dissociate himself from racial particularism, which, in a universalistic courtroom, could only be construed as bias. But in doing so, he risked his status as an authentic black man—and in the race man ideology, to be an authentic black man is to put the black race first.

These contradictory gods don't just occupy the courtroom. In this high-tech economy, universalistic standards of merit, which can be quantified, have become increasingly important, making decisions based on racial considerations more flagrant. That new immigrants of color are often educated and are able to negotiate job hierarchies that were closed to blacks seemingly puts the lie to the suggestion that qualified people of color are barred from these positions and reinforces the belief of some that it is blacks themselves who are to blame, rather than the system. The reality, however, is that the progress of incorporating blacks into mainstream American life has slowed, for the middle class as well as for the underclass. Jobs that would have led to incorporation have vanished, forcing people to adapt or die.

Blacks often see these events as reflecting the racism of a white population that has always discouraged their demands for fuller inclusion and participation in the wider society's economic, political, and social life, and they respond by embracing their own ethnic particularism. Unfortunately, the line between ethnocentrism and alienation can be blurry. Whether young blacks are of the street or of the middle class, it is hard for them to see themselves as part of the wider society. At black colleges and other black institutions, young people display elements of the street culture simply to prove to others that they're truly black and haven't sold out, that they haven't forgotten their roots. Most young African Americans ultimately come to terms with these feelings of alienation. Those with fewer resources, however, may express it through drug abuse and violence. Only one of the resulting tragedies of this alienation is the tendency of some whites to discriminate against all blacks because to do otherwise simply requires too much energy and an understanding that they do not possess.

In these circumstances, black men have begun to stir. An overwhelming number of them were willing to be counted in the Million Man March, whatever their feelings about Farrakhan. Clearly, many black men believe that the time has arrived to look seriously at themselves and their experience in America. And in these circumstances, the race man comes home. The fact that the country seems to be turning its back on blacks, cutting off access to the avenues of mobility that the black middle class has come to rely on over the past quarter century serves to reactivate the race man ideology.

The reality that half the people in U.S. prisons are black men also reactivates this ideology. Blacks know from personal experience that they are scrutinized by the police more than whites are—whether walking down the street, driving a car, or holding public office. Blacks are not allowed to "slide" as whites are. When penalized, blacks are told, "We're just going by the rules," but it is common knowledge that the rules are bent more often for whites. Meanwhile, as reported in several newspapers, black juries increasingly seem to be freeing black and minority men. It is a phenomenon that could well be symptomatic of the emergence of a black middle class that is also sympathetic and understanding in a way the white middle class, in general, has not been toward black defendants.

These two factors emerged with particular force in the Simpson case. On the one hand, there was the desire to see a black man triumph over a system that is so often stacked against black men, and on the other hand, there was a heightened sensitivity to the life situations of black men.

As much as we may detest the influence of race and the way that it has created a certain spuriousness in the 1990s in America, it's there. Johnnie Cochran acknowledged that fact, encouraging the jurors to look at race in the society as opposed to just the facts of the case. Black man, white woman, superstar—all played a part.

It could be argued that Cochran was obligated to defend his client by any legal and legitimate means, although assessments of what is legitimate vary from person to person, even within the legal profession. Cochran's defense was to transform Simpson into a symbol of black persecution in a white judicial system that is already distrusted by a large number of blacks. In these times, when the black community is seen to be under assault by the wider society, the community is coming together around the defense of black victims at the same time as it is searching for race men, leaders of the race. In fulfilling this need, Cochran effectively played what whites saw as the race card. However, he was playing with a hand that was dealt him by the circumstances of history, particularly such recent events as

ELIJAH ANDERSON

the Rodney King affair and a whole host of grievances toward the police that had been building up in the black community.

Whether incidentally or intentionally, this defense doomed Darden to be labeled a sellout by forcing him to play a role that is inconsistent with the ideology of the black community. A disturbing implication of all this for American society is that Darden found himself out of style because the prevailing racial atmosphere is one in which the ultimate value of integration and conformity with the larger society is increasingly being called into question.

Elijah Anderson is the Charles and William L. Day Professor of the Social Sciences, profesor of sociology, and director of the Philadelphia Ethnography Project at the University of Pennsylvania. An expert on the sociology of black America, he is the author of the widely regarded sociological work A Place on the Corner: A Study of Black Street Corner Men *(1978), numerous articles on the black experience, and the forthcoming* The Code of the Streets. *For his recently published ethnographic study,* Streetwise: Race, Class and Change in an Urban Community *(1990), he was honored with the Robert E. Park Award by the American Sociological Association. An associate editor of* Qualitative Sociology, *he is a member of the Board of Directors of the American Academy of Political and Social Science.*

Black Challenge/White Justice

ANDREA FORD

When I phoned to get a racial breakdown of the staff of the Los Angeles district attorney's office, the requested numbers were immediately faxed to my desk. When I asked for similar racial statistics on the 350,000 criminal cases the office handles each year, the response was also quick. It just wasn't useful.

"We try to remain pretty color blind here," Suzanne Childs, spokeswoman for District Attorney Gil Garcetti, said pleasantly.

Was she kidding? No, I was assured.

Funny. I've never thought of anything that goes on in Los Angeles's criminal justice system as color blind. In fact, the one thing that has always struck me about that system is what has appeared to be a strict racial hierarchy, dominated—numerically at least—by whites. In

Garcetti's office, for instance, as the statistics Childs sent me showed, nearly 76 percent of the 1,000 lawyers were white. Garcetti's executive staff was all white. Similarly, the vast majority of the 236 judges on the Los Angeles Superior Court are white, as are the court administrators. This is the racial breakdown in a county where 60 percent of the residents are not white, where almost everyone agrees that the vast majority of the defendants who are prosecuted and judged are people of color.

This was without question true in the Criminal Courts Building in downtown Los Angeles, where for three years I covered the prosecutor's office and trials, including the O. J. Simpson criminal case, for the *Los Angeles Times*. Typical defendants there were brown or black and poor, often hauled into court in chains, sullen or resigned in their jailhouse jumpers and jailhouse braids. Someone dubbed them the "No Js" during the "Trial of the Century."

To a black woman like me, it was not a place to go to get uplifted. Often it was downright frightening because of what I perceived to be an atmosphere in which racial insensitivity and outright antiblack sentiment bubbled just below the surface. I recall once almost colliding with two white police detectives at the entrance to the court-house. After I slipped in ahead of them and walked toward the elevators, I heard someone behind me singing, "Hey, hey, she's a monkey" to the tune of the theme song of the old *Monkees* television show. When I wheeled around, the two white cops were standing there with the most evil smirks on their faces. If this is the way they treated me, I thought, a total stranger who could have been a presidential appointee for all they knew, how did they treat the suspects they brought into court to be prosecuted?

On another occasion, I sat in on a scheduling hearing in a racially charged case in which a white bouncer at a Hollywood bar was charged with gunning down two unarmed black men. To my amazement, the white defense lawyer in the case joked in open court to the white judge about how much "fun" the case would be. Apparently unbeknownst to her, several family members of the victims sat there listening. Later, when the families complained to the presiding judge, they were told that no such remarks appeared in the transcript of the hearing, suggesting that they—and I—were delusional.

It was in this racial milieu that I first encountered Christopher Darden. And it is in this context that I want to discuss the so-called Darden Dilemma, defined by Darden in his best-selling book *In Contempt* as the "pressure that [black prosecutors] feel from those in the community who criticize them for standing up and convicting black criminals." In other forums, Darden has harshly attacked black juries, in general, and the mostly black Simpson jury, in particular, implying that, at best, they exacerbate dilemmas all black prosecutors face.

Let me say from the outset that on the basis of my own observations and on interviews I conducted for this chapter, the validity of Darden's broad assertions is questionable. Such dilemmas may or may not have existed for Darden in the Simpson case, but is his experience applicable to all black prosecutors? I raise this question not to suggest that black criminal justice professionals do not often find themselves dealing with forces that their white counterpoints escape. They are, after all, often among a minority of black people working in white-dominated justice systems that seem to grind the hardest on a large number of black people in this white-dominated society that often equates criminality with blackness.

These factors, in my mind, automatically put them in some kind of a dilemma. But by projecting his unique situation onto others and ignoring and, in some cases, denying the very existence of broader issues, Darden left himself open to criticism. If he had looked beyond himself or, at least, tried to put his experience into a broader context, his credibility would not have been so easily challenged and his grievances might have been taken more seriously. Instead, he insisted and continues to insist that race played no part in his assignment to the Simpson case, to the roles he was assigned as a member of the prosecution team, and in his career in general. For him, the enemy is his own people. Ironically, he has sought to defend what he must know is a flawed system in which race has never *not* mattered.

I first met Darden in 1991, long before Geraldo Rivera and Larry King, million-dollar book deals, and Beverly Hills agents came his way. I identified with him immediately as another black who was working in a system—in my case, the white-dominated news media—that gave off signs of being stacked against some groups, including our own. This perception of him did not spring from my imagination. I covered his first high-profile trial, in which he was pitted, somewhat unfairly, I thought, given the racial and political climate in Los Angeles at the time, against the still politically untouchable, unreformed-and-proud-of-it Los Angeles Police Department (LAPD).

The case involved four white police officers who were charged in the locally infamous Thirty-ninth and Dalton police vandalism case. The charges stemmed from a raid in which eighty cops descended on the residences of four black families in South Central Los Angeles, ostensibly looking for a gang's drug stash. When the raid was over, no more than a few rocks of cocaine had been confiscated (from someone who had no connection to the residences), but the homes had been so trashed that the Red Cross declared them disaster areas. Toilets had been pulled from the floor, washing machines had been thrown out windows, bleach had been poured on clothing, food had been snatched from freezers and tossed outside, stairways had been ripped from their moorings, and "LAPD Rules" had been written on walls.

Darden lost the case. But not after getting into a public, admirably courageous clash with the then still-powerful LAPD chief, Daryl F. Gates. On the basis of private conversations I had with him and others at the time, I know that Darden fully appreciated the difficulty of the role he had been put in by being named to prosecute those cops. In my estimation, he was little more than a sacrificial lamb, expendable in a case that was likely to be unwinnable because of racial politics, a high level of police credibility, and the difficulty of assigning blame to a few officers who may or may not have been guilty of specific criminal actions.

Later, when I moved my office to the press suite in the Criminal Courts Building, one floor up from his office, we talked sometimes. Darden was never one to bare his soul, to me anyway, but he often made remarks that suggested that he was a frustrated black man in a white man's world who was not advancing as fast as he thought he should, solely because of his race. He was as sullen and seemingly conflicted then as he was throughout the Simpson trial. Thus, I reacted with surprise when he so vehemently defended the prosecutor's office as being racially color blind in its assigning him to the Simpson case, especially when the assignment occurred after a heavily black jury had been seated. What person in his or her right mind would not wonder if tokenism was not at play? "I'm not any token here," I recall Darden confidently saying to me in a private conversation after his assignment was announced. "I'm going to be the engineer. I'm going to drive this train."

Perhaps he was. Perhaps he did.

But in my view, nothing he said after the case was over described the complexity of his role in the criminal justice system. To get a broader view of the landscape, I talked to others, all of whom are or have been prosecutors in jurisdictions around the country. Several of those I interviewed appeared in the summer of 1996 on a panel I organized for the annual conference of the National Association of Black Journalists (NABJ), of which I am a member. The question before the panel was whether the so-called Darden Dilemma was real. The five panelists— a former state prosecutor–turned–judge, two elected prosecutors, a former assistant U.S. attorney–turned–legal academic, and a former state prosecutor–turned–defense lawyer—all concluded that it was not real for anyone other than, perhaps, Darden.

For the most part, they talked about the responsibility they felt to tilt the system toward justice and fairness whenever they could and how difficult it can be to do so in some cases. The following are vignettes of some of those who appeared on the NABJ panel, as well as of others, in which they discuss the issues they face as black criminal justice professionals and how they deal with these issues.

Bobby Grace didn't plan to be a prosecutor while growing up in San Bernardino in the eastern section of southern California. He didn't plan not to be one either. He just happened to get a job as a law clerk in the Los Angeles District Attorney's Office while in law school. Once he passed the California bar exam in 1988, the office offered him a job. He has worked there ever since as a deputy district attorney, most recently in the gang unit.

The thirty-six-year-old deputy district attorney hasn't had a case involving a white defendant in five years because, as he put it, *gang* in Los Angeles law-enforcement and criminal-justice circles means black or brown. "White gangs are not assigned to our unit," he said. "I'm sure they're out there [but] they go to [the] hate crimes or organized crime [unit]. If it's white, it's labeled a white-collar crime." Outside the gang unit, he said, most of the defendants in Los Angeles County's courts are also black and brown.

Grace attributes that fact to the demographics of Los Angeles County, socioeconomic factors, and selective arrest patterns. "There's pressure on the police from City Hall and community people themselves to do something about street crime," he said. "Street crime is out in the open, and it usually is committed by black or brown people. That doesn't mean that whites don't commit crimes. They are just more insulated and less likely to be arrested, less likely to present the stereotype of what a criminal should look like and less likely to be sentenced harshly."

In explaining the fact that whites are less likely to be

sentenced harshly, Grace suggested that racism plays a lesser role than does economics. "Whites are more likely to be able to hire their own lawyers, which makes a big difference [in] how a case is handled throughout the process," he said. "Money drives the criminal justice system just like it does everything else. If you have your own lawyer, everybody in the courtroom stands up and takes notice. If you don't, it's just another run-of-the-mill case, and it will be treated as run of the mill."

Because of that situation, Grace believes, African Americans inside the criminal justice system have a responsibility to their community to use their influence to alleviate such disparities. For a line prosecutor, he said, that influence can be significant because prosecutors are given discretion in deciding which cases to file, whether to file cases as misdemeanors or felonies, whether to plea bargain, and whether to recommend prison time and how much. "These are areas where there have been charges that African Americans are not treated the same as white defendants, where white defendants get the benefit of the doubt," he noted. Without apology, Grace said that he consciously tries to give black offenders the same benefit of the doubt. If there is a conviction in a case, he said, he tries to work out a mutually agreeable recommendation for a sentence with the defense lawyer.

Grace denies that this is pro-black bias. He calls it fairness, adding that he has never been pressured by his white colleagues and supervisors to do otherwise. Nor has he, he contended, been pressured by black people to go easy on black defendants, as a *Wall Street Journal* article on him in the winter of 1996 suggested. The article, "Facing the Darden Dilemma," portrayed Grace as a victim of the phenomenon. It was published after he had been brought in to assist a white prosecutor in the prosecution of the rapper Snoop Doggy Dogg and his bodyguard for murder. Both defendants were eventually acquitted of taking part in a fatal drive-by shooting. In one scene in the *Wall Street Journal* article, the reporter depicted Grace walking a gauntlet of black fans of Snoop Doggy Dogg.

"You know they're judging you," the article quoted Grace as saying. In his interview with me, Grace said he was referring to the rapper's family and friends, whom, he said, one would expect to be hostile toward him. Black people who were not close to the case and who contacted him were supportive, he stressed.

That's not to say that Grace is not sometimes asked about his career choice. "It's usually people who do not live in the 'hood'," he said. "They are not aware of the level of violent crime being perpetrated on our people."

Color-blind justice is not something Roosevelt F. Dorn has ever encountered in his twenty-seven years as a city prosecutor and judge.

"Never seen it. Never heard of it. Never heard of anyone who has heard of it," he joked as he sat in his chambers in Inglewood, a largely black suburb of Los Angeles, where he is legendary for his no-nonsense approach to juvenile justice. It is said that the only way for a youngster to get off Dorn-imposed probation is to die or graduate from high school.

The Superior Court judge has been known to keep youths on probation for years, requiring them to make frequent, in-person progress reports; go to school every day; and maintain a C average. Defiance means a swift order for incarceration. Cops, school officials, and parents who have lost control of their offspring love the sixty-one-year-old jurist.

Some lawyers don't. Public defenders who find their cases assigned to him routinely "paper" him or exercise their onetime right to reject a judge without having to give an explanation. They describe Dorn as well meaning but overzealous, maintaining ironfisted control over the lives of young people long after they have paid their debt to society. Such criticism doesn't bother Dorn, who believes his tough approach has made a "tremendous difference" with youngsters who were headed down the wrong road and who were abandoned by the overworked and sometimes uncaring probationary system. He gets his reward, he said, when those young people, some of whom hadn't been to school for a year or more when they came under his jurisdiction, come to his courtroom to show him their high school diplomas.

He could not have made such an impact, Dorn said,

in the adult Criminal Court in downtown Los Angeles, where he presided in a sort of exile for four years between 1989 and 1993 as the result of what he contends was a racially motivated dispute with a juvenile court administrator. "Most of the people who came through" his downtown courtroom "already had felony records and were on their way to the penitentiary. There isn't a lot you can do for them."

It was while he was serving in the Criminal Court, however, that Dorn publicly locked horns with Ira Reiner, then the district attorney of Los Angeles County, and eventually made it back to his first love, Juvenile Court. The dispute with Reiner stemmed from the district attorney's refusal to allow Dorn to hear the case that became a symbol of the 1992 Los Angeles riots—the trial of three black men who were accused of dragging white truck driver Reginald Denny from his vehicle and beating him senseless as a television helicopter crew filmed the scene. Dorn had been handpicked to hear the case by a court administrator who candidly acknowledged that race was a factor in the choice, since Dorn was then the only black judge sitting in the downtown Criminal Courts Building.

Reiner exercised his right to reject Dorn, he said at first, because Dorn's calendar was overloaded. When Dorn held a press conference and called Reiner a liar, the district attorney stated that the real reason was that questions had been raised about Dorn's ability to get along with others. Dorn won't say that Reiner's action was racially motivated, but many others did. Blacks throughout the Los Angeles area, who had been generally supportive of Reiner, rushed to defend Dorn. Some of the most prominent black ministers in the city denounced Reiner from their pulpits.

The district attorney, who was at the time in the midst of a bitter reelection campaign that pitted him against former aide Gil Garcetti, soon withdrew from the race. The following year, after winning accolades for his performance in the adult court, Dorn returned to Juvenile Court in Inglewood, where he wants to be. He credits his ability to withstand attacks against him to his close ties to the black community, something he believes all black professionals must maintain to be effective in white-dominated work environments.

In a flawed and sometimes discriminatory criminal justice system, African Americans can and should make a difference, he maintains, rather than pretend they don't see bias. "I tell young lawyers all the time that if they really want to be in a position to help their people, to be there when they need you, the greatest place in the world to be is in the prosecutor's office," he said. "When you think equity should be done in a case or you think a particular defendant should have some type of break, you're in a position to give it to him. You can't do that if you stand back and never become a part of the system. It's very difficult to fight the system from the outside."

■　　　　■　　　　■

When then–Cuyahoga County prosecutor John T. Corrigan resigned in 1990, ending a thirty-four-year reign, most people expected him to be succeeded by his son. But the county Democratic Party had other ideas. It voted to appoint Stephanie Tubbs Jones to fill out his term. The former assistant prosecutor had served as a judge on both the Cleveland Municipal Court and the Cuyahoga County Common Pleas Court and before that was a trial lawyer in the Cleveland office of the Equal Employment Opportunity Commission.

The year after her appointment as county prosecutor, Jones was officially elected to the post with a whopping 70 percent of the vote in a county where blacks make up just 25 percent of the population. Black folks in and around Cleveland, where Jones grew up, were elated. Some weren't happy, however, when she issued a subpoena to Cleveland's black mayor as part of an investigation of suspected wrongdoing in the construction of a housing complex. The subpoena was delivered at a conference of black mayors that happened to be meeting in the city at the time. Some black folks accused Jones of deliberately trying to embarrass the mayor because he was black.

On the other side of the coin, some whites have questioned Jones's ability to be fair and to investigate and prosecute black elected officials vigorously. Her response is, "If white people can be fair prosecuting white people, I can be fair prosecuting black people."

Jones will be the last to tell you that in her position,

she is free of pressures to please one racial constituency or another. "I'm conscious of it in every decision I make," she said, "but I've made the decision not to fall to the pressure."

She is also aware, however, that she's the only elected black prosecutor in Ohio. Therefore, she said, she believes she has an obligation to be a spokesperson for "people of color." "I don't ever want to walk away from being a black person and a woman. People of color in public office do have a special obligation" to level the playing field, she noted. "If they are unwilling to accept that responsibility, then they shouldn't be in office."

To maintain credibility in her community, she said, she has a heavy speaking schedule, so people will know something about her other than what appears in newspaper headlines. To outflank her critics, she is always prepared to justify her decisions and to challenge stereotypes that dog black officeholders. For instance, when she was first appointed to her position, she realized that some people viewed her as soft on crime. Therefore, she went back into the courtroom to try a case so her constituents could see her in action. For the case, which involved a black defendant who was accused of killing a white woman, Jones sought the death penalty. She later prosecuted a white man who was accused of killing an interracial couple and also sought the death penalty.

Her greatest impact, she believes, has been in bringing more diversity to her staff. When she first took over the office, she said, there was one black investigator on the staff, 10 black assistant prosecutors, and no black members of the 80-member support staff. Six years later, 26 of her 140 assistant prosecutors are black, and there are 30 black members of her support staff. "This is a public office, and it should reflect and give access to all people," Jones asserted, adding that a significant number of the crime victims her office sees are black. Having a respectable number of black faces in the office gives those victims "a certain comfort level," she noted.

Jones is under no illusion that she alone can correct what she views as deep-seated racial inequities in the criminal justice system. "The criminal justice system is just a microcosm of our society," she said. "We didn't get to where we are in a day, and we cannot cure what's wrong in a day. All I can do is continue to put in place policies that address the inequities."

John Burris remembers when it became clear to him that he couldn't continue to be a deputy district attorney in Alameda County in the San Francisco Bay Area. He had gone to a judge to recommend a sentence in a simple case of marijuana possession in which the defendant was a young black man.

"I had some deal for a thirty- to ninety-day sentence, thinking that was fair," Burris said. "The judge looked at me and said, 'We don't talk days here. We talk years.'"

The encounter, said Burris, drove home to him something he had always suspected—that many of the white prosecutors and judges he worked with were unwilling to give black male defendants a break even when a break was warranted.

He had heard it in the office banter. He had seen it in the patterns of who got charged with what crimes and who got the deals. He sometimes felt he was in a room full of unforgiving cops. "There was a harshness and a lack of sensitivity on a day-to-day basis" when it came to black defendants, Burris remarked. "If [a prosecutor] had a choice of giving a felony or a misdemeanor, they would go for the felony. I knew a felony could have a detrimental affect on the rest of the person's life."

Burris stated that he handled the situation by focusing on his main purpose for being in the office—getting trial experience so he could strike out on his own. He sympathizes with young black prosecutors or other black professionals who find themselves in environments in which biases against black people are evident. The question, he said, is, What do you do to distance yourself from those attitudes or to correct them? "Sometimes you can't see it. You deal with your cases and do not see the inequities going on. You can buy into the process. When you're on the inside, it's easy to do that."

Other times, Burris observed, you see what's going on and have to decide what you're going to do about it. Outspokenness, he said, comes with its own risks, particularly if you are young and new in your career. He chose to get out of that line of lawyering.

Burris became a defense lawyer and now has a civil practice in San Francisco, where most of his cases involve police misconduct. He believes he is more effective fighting racial and other kinds of injustice in that capacity. He acted as one of Rodney King's lawyers in the federal trial in which two of the four accused police officers were convicted of violating King's civil rights. He is currently representing a six-year-old black boy who is accused of beating a baby after he and two eight year olds broke into a neighbor's house. The authorities wanted to try the child as an adult—a decision that would not even have been considered if the boy had been white, Burris believes.

Of his stint as a prosecutor, he said: "I ran from the process because I was tired of seeing all those black boys going to jail. I didn't want to be a part of it. I thought there were other areas where I could do other things." He wouldn't necessarily recommend the same course of action to other black lawyers who want to be prosecutors.

"Number one, it's a good job. Everyone doesn't want to be in private practice," he said. Being a prosecutor is "a secure position and an opportunity to do public service." Moreover, he said, black prosecutors can make a difference in providing a level of sensitivity for victims, who, in many jurisdictions, are often black. "That's what fired me up as a prosecutor," he noted. "I saw a level of insincerity with [some] white prosecutors when they were dealing with black victims. They'd talk to them disrespectfully. They'd make them wait. They'd have them come to the courthouse when there was no need for them to be there. They'd also be disrespectful to [black] witnesses. Those things bothered me. I saw them happening on an ongoing basis."

In Detroit, Kym Worthy was known as much for her caustic I-will-not-suffer-fools manners as for her prosecutorial skills until she started racking up a string of victories that nobody could ignore. Included among the six hundred cases she prosecuted with a 90 percent conviction rate was that of a woman who had been charged with killing her husband upon his return from the Persian Gulf War, a case that had originally captured the nation's attention as a symbol of random violence.

When in 1993 Worthy won the convictions of two white police officers who were accused of using their flashlights to beat to death an unarmed black suspect named Malice Green, the word on her was that she was an ascending star. Less than two years later, she was elected a judge in Detroit Recorder's Court. As a prosecutor and a judge, Worthy said, she has gotten nothing but support from the crime-weary residents of a city she described as "the blackest" in the country. "When you talk about crime here, you're talking about almost all black defendants and all black victims," she said.

Perhaps because of that situation, Worthy has trouble understanding the notion that black professionals in the criminal justice system are resented by other black people because they participate in a system that sometimes is viewed as unfair to black people. In her experience, she stated, she has seen no such thing. "My experience has been that black people are eager and glad when they see black prosecutors. They know no stone will be unturned. Nobody has ever called me an Uncle Tom. I have never been made to feel uncomfortable. If anything, people could see I brought a special sensitivity to a case."

But even in a city as black as Detroit, Worthy noted, inequities exist in the criminal justice system. Blacks continue to draw harsher charges than whites and are less likely to be offered alternatives to time behind bars. As an African American prosecutor, she said, "I felt a special responsibility to address racism. I never saw that as an extra burden. It is my responsibility as a human being to do what is right. If that means sending an African American to prison for a long time, it's not a pleasant thing and it doesn't make me happy, but someone who kills and robs shouldn't be out there on the street."

Her loyalties, she said, are reserved for those residents who choose to be law abiding. That doesn't mean, she said, that she doesn't advocate for programs for nonviolent and first-time offenders that keep them from getting sucked deeply into the criminal justice system. "The most important thing in my mind is getting those cases that don't belong there out of the system." As a prosecutor and a judge, especially a black prosecutor and a judge, she believes, her role is to help "balance the scales of justice."

Andrea Ford, an award-winning journalist, has been a reporter at the Los Angeles Times *for nearly a decade and was one of the* Times*'s lead reporters on the O. J. Simpson double-murder trial. As a Metro staffer at the* Times, *she shared a Pulitzer Prize and a George Polk Award for coverage of the 1992 Los Angeles riots and was honored for her coverage of the riot by the* Los Angeles Sentinel *and the* Los Angeles Press Club. *In 1995, she was named Journalist of the Year by the National Association of Black Journalists for her work on the Simpson trial. A Detroit native, she began her career at the* Detroit Free Press.

Outside Players
CLARENCE PAGE

I'd known from the beginning, from the moment I walked into that courtroom a year earlier and saw that jury. I could see in their eyes the need to settle some score. And I was the only prosecutor who knew what the score was.
— CHRISTOPHER DARDEN, *In Contempt*

Everyone talks about "the O. J. trial," but actually there were two trials. There was the inside trial, in which O. J. Simpson was the defendant, and there was an outside trial, in which America's system of justice was the defendant. The inside trial, carefully controlled by rules of procedure and evidence, was less complicated than the outside trial, in which there were no limits on facts, rumors, hearsay, conjecture, and, most tellingly, personal experiences. "The life of the law has not been logic: It has been experience," wrote Oliver Wendell Holmes Jr., which makes interpositions of race and law even more vexing, since all our racial experiences are so different. This begins to explain why, even before the inside trial's opening gavel, a poll showed that two-thirds of white Americans already thought

Simpson was guilty, while two-thirds of black Americans thought he was not guilty, if not totally innocent. We dare not make too much of such polls. Not guilty is not quite the same as innocent. But we dare not make too little of them, either.

Why? Because for better or for worse, individuals' beliefs about Simpson's guilt or innocence say a great deal about those individuals' faith (or lack thereof) in the American system of justice. Many of those who said they thought O. J. was guilty were saying that they hoped the system worked. They hoped it would never have charged an O. J. Simpson in the first place unless he was guilty. Many who thought O. J. was not guilty were saying, in effect, that they knew good and well that the system was seriously flawed, especially when it came to black men. *"Sure, I know the system doesn't work because my uncle got arrested and beat up by the cops the other night and he ain't done nothin'!"* *"And a black man married to a white woman, too? Fair trial? You mus' be crazy!"*

If experience is not always the best teacher, it certainly is the most persuasive, and such experiences as the aforementioned can fuel a lifetime of distrust. Even one bad experience, as we all know, can alter our point of view, and most African Americans can claim more than one such encounter with a prejudiced system. "A conservative," according to a slogan of a the post-'60s era, "is only a liberal who's been mugged." Tom Wolfe, in his novel *The Bonfire of the Vanities*, offered a corollary: "A liberal is only a conservative who's been arrested." Black Americans, generally speaking, are more likely to have had personal experiences that lend less credibility to the justice system, from the cop on the street to the Supreme Court, than white people have had. White Americans, again speaking generally, are more likely to trust the system, since members of their race have had a larger part in constructing and maintaining it. So just as there was an inside trial and an outside trial, those who followed the trial could be labeled as either insiders or outsiders, depending on their views of the justice system.

Unlike whites, who, no matter what their class and education, can claim a certain insider status if only because of their more acceptable skin color, blacks more often than not may be described as outsiders because of the black psychological and existential condition in this white-dominated society. One can glory in the feeling or wallow in sorrow over it, but one cannot easily escape it. The relaxing of formal segregation since the 1950s and 1960s has opened up black opportunities for advancement, but has done little to ease blacks' anxieties and doubts about white people—even though, ironically, it *has* succeeded in assuaging the white guilt that has been history's most potent force for black advancement. Because of this lingering anxiety, there was a quiet rejoicing beyond description over the unmasking of Mark Fuhrman's racism and, by association, the system's guilt on national television. Like the

Winfrey, or Colin Powell into their pantheon of whole-some superheroes, black America seemed just as eager to hold onto its claim that he was one of *us*, a homeboy who made good the best way he could, but who was still vulnerable to racist cops and the duplicitous, easily manipulated, justice system. Sitting beneath the unblinking gaze of television cameras, fingered like a modern-day Bigger Thomas for the killing of a white woman, he was transformed instantly from the ultimate insider into a glowing symbol of the black community's shared sense of outsiderness, just another brother on lockdown. If black America did not give him every ben-efit of its doubt, when so many others appeared ready to string him up, who else would?

Thus, Simpson's trial became a test of the racism that many black Americans see all around them every day, a racism most white Americans would rather not talk about, let alone confront. After students at historically black Howard University law school were shown on network television news jumping out of their seats to cheer the not-guilty verdict, one student remarked that it was refreshing to see that a black man had achieved enough wealth to afford "rich white man's justice." In this perverse sense, they saw progress.

But Darden, the man who was trying to put another man in jail, also knew how it felt to be an outsider. He grew up in segregation. He had been stopped by police, like so many of us, for the crime of "driving while black." Yet, like other black prosecutors, he also had enough faith in the judicial system to want to get inside it, to try to make it work for him and for his community.

In my early days as a crime reporter in the 1970s, I quickly learned that prosecutors are wary of "heater" cases—cases that draw an extraordinary amount of public attention and "heat." With Simpson, Darden found himself in modern history's biggest heater case, and his seemingly noble effort quickly put him at odds with those who believe that the system is too irredeemably rotten, too irreversibly dedicated to the subjugation of blacks, to be reformed. By his own accounts, Darden, the aspiring insider, suddenly found himself an outsider in the black community whose interests he was trying to serve.

I sympathized with him. I also criticized him. Because while I was part of the minority of black Americans who thought, based on what I could see of the outside trial, that Simpson probably was guilty, I also thought that the prosecution team failed to prove their case beyond a reasonable doubt against an excellent defense team. O. J. didn't have to speak; he only had to spend money. It is, for better or worse, the American way of justice.

Still, I found myself hoping, in those final suspense-filled minutes, for a "guilty" verdict. I almost prayed for it, if only to confound the cynical voices who insisted that a mostly black jury was incapable of finding a black man guilty, as if our prisons were not overflowing with black men put in them by black jurors. I particularly wanted to silence, if only for a sweet stunning moment, the racists who have used this canard somehow to lessen the sins of white jurors who have aided and abetted the lynching of black men. *"It is the Niggers that are Racists: Not the White Men,"* began one of the many letters Darden received. I wanted to silence those who would suggest that blacks were complicit in an unjust legal system to rob us of our most potent survival tool: white guilt.

But it was not to be. The verdict was not guilty. The prosecution's evidence and argument had failed to do the job. The prosecutors left just enough holes in their argument, which, in the absence of a confession, a murder weapon, or clearly conclusive evidence, formed a kind of inkblot test upon which each observer could lay his or her own stock of experiences and prejudices. Where you stand depends on where you sit—on the inside, believing in the fairness of our system of justice, or on the outside, knowing the system is less than perfect, even deeply flawed when it comes to guaranteeing the rights of long-oppressed minorities. For this reason, O. J. was a symbol even before the trial began.

But although many in the black community immediately pardoned O. J. in their own minds as a black man persecuted in the white man's system (an outsider) and vilified Darden as a black man working for the white man's system (a wannabe insider), reality in the black community is more complex than this duality would suggest. After all, discrimination has declined. Doors have opened up. African Americans are gaining power and access to power in all areas of the establishment. After years of marching with our "eyes on the prize," for many of us the prize has come. Many now worry that outsiderness can be a self-fulfilling prophecy for those who shy away from taking advantage of these new opportunities. Has the time come for us to stop regarding ourselves as outsiders? Will it ever come?

Many will view the question as a naive conceit. How can we even remotely call ourselves "insiders," they will say, when taxis still shun middle-class black businessmen? When police abuses and "glass ceilings" persist? When black home buyers must jump through extra hoops to get home loans? When the nation is awash in a conservative backlash against affirmative action? When the most feared creature on urban streets is the young black man?

The conversation is clouded by differences in perception. Many whites like to think blacks have equal access to the "inside" in the age of Oprah, Cosby, Powell, and the two Michaels (Jordan and Jackson). Whites tend to see, conveniently enough, just enough progress to let them off the hook, to free them of any further obligation to help bring more progress about. Many blacks, in contrast, downplay any progress we have made, either because they don't believe it's significant or because they don't want to let white America off the hook too easily.

Indeed, more than half of African Americans feel

conditions are getting worse for them, according to a survey that Yankelovich Partners conducted for a special "Black in America" issue of *The New Yorker* in 1996. Broken down along class lines, two-thirds of African Americans who belong to the lower class, 57 percent of the working class, 58 percent of the middle class, and 50 percent of the upper middle class and above said that they thought things are getting worse. Overall, half believed that race relations will "never be better than they are," and 59 percent (including 58 percent of the middle class and 49 percent of the upper middle class and above) agreed that the American Dream has become impossible for most Americans to achieve.

"I would argue strongly against the notion that discrimination has diminished," a young black lawyer argued with me at a meeting of young black professionals, organized by the Washington regional National Urban League. "It has only become more subtle. White people always throw up the Colin Powells and Bill Cosbys in your face," he said, "but our law firm only has four black lawyers in it. How can I call myself an insider when, if I was white, I'd be a partner by now?"

Sure, I responded, and if I was white, I'd probably be a publisher by now. Most of my audience, including my young questioner, laughed. As young black professionals in a city where blacks are in the numerical majority yet whites hold most of the money and power, they understood my attempt at irony. Of course, none of us could say for certain how different our lives would have been had we not been born black in white America. Upward mobility isn't easy to achieve, whatever your color may be. Everyone who attempts the long, arduous climb out of poverty and obscurity into the limelight of success must battle all manner of doubts about his or her ability to succeed and the ability of others to be fair. But my audience understood that if we know anything for certain, it is that blackness is a disadvantage in a culture that rewards whiteness, that even in these, the best of our times in America, it brings much doubt and sometimes pain about where we stand with white people. Clinging to the bright light of hope offered these days by a civil society that, for all its flaws, appears to be seeking a peaceful resolution of its past and is grasping for reassurance that its melting pot still works even for people of color, we also are relentlessly pounded by the minefields of daily insults—the store buzzers, the taxi passbys, the *Bell Curves*, the David Dukes, and the Mark Fuhrmans.

Reinforcing our doubts about the fairness of others is the backward tug of self-doubt. The resulting stresses help explain why some psychologists are finding, contrary to the holes of a seemingly racially enlightened age, that it is those of us who have moved the farthest and the fastest who feel the pain of racism most acutely, if only because we have more daily interaction with people of other races. While one must have faith in the fairness of the system to attempt to succeed in it, the effort makes us more vulnerable to disappointment. The committed outsider, stubbornly rejecting the American apple pies as "rotten to the core," as Black Power pioneer Stokely Carmichael (a.k.a. Kwame Toure) said in the 1960s, relieves himself or herself of the possibility of being hurt. Outsiderness, in itself, would seem to have certain advantages to one's state of mind, regardless of how well off or badly off African Americans may happen to be. Like the cat who jumped on a hot stove and then never jumped on a stove, whether hot or cold, again, the outsider finds a certain level of comfort in refusing even to make the effort.

Outsiderness, by its nature, works against assimilation into the mainstream, which is not necessarily bad if the mainstream's values are corrupt or decadent. The outsider may only be noticing this corruption more quickly than insiders do. The intellectual, Edward Said wrote in his *Representations of the Intellectual*, is by nature an outsider, one who "belongs on the side of the weak and underrepresented." Standing with the weak is ennobling. But it must also be admitted that the mere fact that our persistent outsidership is so annoying to white Americans, including the rich and powerful, is its own reward to many black Americans. We can be so fond of this posture that we reflexively suspect anyone who gains the favor of white people too quickly. Powell's popularity was higher among whites than among blacks for many months while the world waited to find out what he believed. White Americans as a group in the 1990s are so desperate for a black hero that his personal beliefs seemed unimportant. Black Americans, vulnerable and wounded by racial turncoats in the past, could not afford that luxury.

Given enough time and rope, outsiders inevitably form in-groups of their own that can mimic the worst excesses of those who previously cast them out. For example, there is the "crabs in the basket" syndrome: When we see one of our fellows trying to escape, we reach out our claws and pull him or her back down. Just ask the striving African American student who has been put down by his friends for "talkin' white" or "actin' white" or the middle-class upwardly mobile professional who winces when he or she hears the word *buppie*. We have failed to sort out and appreciate the positive, life-affirming models of family and community support that sustained African Americans through times much harder than these. To our youths who see success as "white" and, by connection, failure as black, we have failed to offer more than a truncated version of blackness. We have failed, for example, to point out that there is nothing more African than trigonometry, which began with the builders of the great pyramids. Instead, we have completed the racist's work by embracing stereotypes and expelling our brightest minds who failed to meet a faulty community standard.

It is with this voice, the voice of the double outsider, cast out by outcasts, with which Darden speaks when he writes, "Perhaps I had to be 'kicked out' of the black community to understand my place in it. But sometimes the view is much better from outside." Darden is caught in a double bind from which he is trying to draw some measure of strength. As an outsider who came inside the system, he finds himself ostracized by the "community" he is trying to help. Yet, he finds the experience to be enlightening. "Suffering is redemptive," said Martin Luther King Jr. Sometimes the view is better from the outside.

And sometimes it is not. The outsider mentality, with all its suspicions and resentments, probably played a decisive role in the thinking of the Simpson jurors. Some particularly petulant critics have taken that as a sign that the system has broken down, that blacks are too angry to be good jurors, as if anger at the system had no role to play in correcting the flaws of that system. Quite the contrary, if the angry outsider has no other avenues through which to express his or her grievances—if the legislators are unyielding, the chief executive is not listening, and the corporate world is not caring, the outsider will exert power though whatever avenue is available, even the jury system. "No justice, no peace," charged the protesters outside the Simpson court. To ensure lasting peace, the outsider's voice must not be suppressed. It must be heard. It must be engaged. It must be given a place at the table. Only then can the outsider be brought inside and the cycle of pain be broken. Then it will be up to us, the traditional insiders, to respond. It may be too early for African Americans to start thinking of themselves as insiders.

But it is not too early for us to start thinking about thinking about it.

Clarence Page, a syndicated columnist for the Chicago Tribune *and author of* Showing My Color: Impolite Essays on Race and Identity *(HarperCollins, 1996) won the Pulitzer Prize for commentary in 1989. He is a frequent voice on National Public Radio's* Sunday Morning Edition, *a regular commentator on* The NewsHour with Jim Lehrer *and* The MacLaughlin Group, *and a weekly panelist on Black Entertainment Television's* Lead Story. *He has contributed to the* New Republic *and the* Wall Street Journal, *among other publications.*

Moon's Paradox

ANITA HILL

In the beginning, theirs was like a fairy-tale romance. He was the gifted quarterback. She was the spirited cheerleader who made up cheers especially for him and taught them to the rest of the squad. Even after seventeen years of marriage, when they appeared together on the *Larry King Live* show, Warren and Felicia Moon could have been the models for a wedding-cake adornment. Both were still beautiful despite the ugliness in their marriage that she had relived before a courtroom filled with journalists who were anxious to get to the truth. Was Warren Moon a wife beater in the privacy of his home, or was he, as his public reputation suggested, the "good guy" of professional football? Felicia Moon had the unenviable task of informing us all which of the two images was true. Her role, in a legal sense, was simple. She had only to tell the truth about what happened on July 18, 1995, that led to Warren Moon's arrest for spousal assault. But in a larger social context, her role was anything but simple. Felicia Moon had to sort out all interests, perspectives, and truths presented by the situation and determine what was the "whole truth . . . and nothing but the truth"—one that the jury and the public would believe. Certainly, individuals like Christopher Darden inevitably weigh community sentiment in making professional decisions. But what the Moon case illustrates is that community sentiment often influences intimate personal choices as well. When the personal details of one's marriage are brought into the public arena, the potential for conflict and confusion is compounded. Questions about what is private and what is public, as well as which is self-interest and which is community interest, get decided under the glare of television cameras. Yet what goes into the decision-making process rarely gets a public airing.

From the scene at Warren and Felicia Moon's home on July 18, 1995, to the press conference and emotional testimony that followed, the entire episode can be characterized all too easily as a modern morality play. The question on which the jury ultimately had to pass judgment was not unlike those raised on popular talk shows—the successors to the soap operas that were popular in the 1970s and 1980s. The soap opera viewer could feel self-righteous relief knowing that she or he had not made as much a mess of things as the soap opera writers could possibly imagine. Similarly, in the realm of talk shows, each day the television audience becomes a jury of popular consensus that is asked to respond to questions such as, "Does your mother dress like a tramp?" or "Should you take your man back after he sleeps with your best friend?" Though they sometimes blur the distinction between reality and entertainment, we expect that talk shows will have few real consequences, barely more than their fictional counterparts. Unlike the Jenny Jones show guest who was so embarrassed by a show's content that he killed a fellow participant, guests leave the shows and are free to live their lives as they please regardless of the audience's verdict or reaction.

The media coverage of Warren Moon's arrest provided the perfect antidote for a public that was tired of the artificiality of soap operas and the inconsequentiality of the talk shows. Moon's case involved real drama—pain and anguish, the true lives of celebrities, someone whom we thought we knew—and real consequences. And via the press, the public was treated to the play start to finish without commercial interruptions.

According to the police in Missouri City, Texas, where the Moons live, the actual events of the opening scene were all too common to present-day society: Husband and wife quarrel; husband physically attacks wife. A member of the household calls the police to the scene. Another instance of domestic violence. Today, much in contrast to the past, such episodes often result in the husband's arrest for assault.

But Felicia and Warren Moon's story offered more drama than a simple assault charge might suggest. On July 18, 1995, after a period of estrangement, the couple argued. In fact, they quarreled so loudly that they frightened their seven-year-old son and their housekeeper. When it became apparent to the housekeeper that the quarrel had escalated from shouting to a physical altercation, she dialed 911 and handed the telephone to the child, who alerted the emergency dispatcher. "My daddy is going to hit my mommy. Please hurry!"

Felicia Moon fled the house in one car, and Warren Moon pursued her in another through their residential neighborhood, sometimes traveling at speeds in excess of seventy-five miles per hour. After both Moons left their home, police officers arrived and talked to the child and the housekeeper. They remained at the home until Felicia Moon returned without Warren Moon. She explained to the police that she and her husband had fought and that he had strangled her to the point where she "saw black." According to Mrs. Moon, she fled the house in fear of her life, and her husband had pursued her. There had been a chase, but she had eluded him and returned home. Though she did not want to press charges against him at the time, she did allow the police to take pictures of her scratches and the bruises on her neck that she said were a result of the attack.

Four days later, Mrs. Moon and a contrite Mr. Moon

appeared together in a press conference—a public con-fessional for him. "Things had gotten out of hand" between him and his wife. He was sorry and was taking steps to ensure that this incident would never be repeated. Hours later, local authorities arrested Mr. Moon and charged him with a misdemeanor assault punishable by up to a year in prison and a fine of $4,000.

As time passed, Felicia Moon became adamant that she did not want to charge her husband with criminal assault or testify against him in a criminal proceeding. The prosecutor was equally adamant and unpersuaded by what seemed now to be Felicia Moon's resistance to the charges that she herself had made. According to the district attorney's version of the drama, Mrs. Moon was like many victims of domestic violence. A large percent-age, as many as 50 percent, of women who seek help from the police later refuse to press charges or recant their stories, some on the eve of the trials. They may do so out of fear of retaliation or on the basis of a promised or hoped-for reconciliation. Even without Felicia Moon's cooperation, though, District Attorney John Healey continued to pursue the assault charge against Warren Moon. Moreover, prosecutors invoked a Texas law waiving spousal immunity and issued a subpoena to force Felicia Moon to testify at Warren Moon's trial. He subpoenaed the Moons' seven-year-old son as well.

On the day the trial was to begin, Felicia Moon fled with her son. After some negotiation via car telephone, she agreed to return in exchange for Warren Moon's assurance that he would not enter into a plea bargain with the district attorney's office. She would later tell the press that she didn't want her children to see their father as a criminal.

Thus, the tone of the trial was set. The choice to testify or not, which Felicia Moon had attempted to avoid, was forced on her. A choice of what she would testify to remained. The trial, which was supposed to be about whether Warren Moon was a batterer, now focused on another question entirely.

Just as the press conference following the initial news story was Warren Moon's confessional, the trial became Felicia Moon's confessional. According to her description of herself, she was a spendthrift prone to fits of rage and often depressed during their troubled marriage. She described the physical difficulties she experienced with one of her pregnancies and how she took her unhappiness out on her husband, even refusing to have sex with him on occasion. Yes, she knew that he had been unfaithful to her, but she had forgiven him. On the day that the couple's seven-year-old child spoke to the 911 operator, she testified, it was she who started the violence by throwing a candleholder at her husband. The housekeeper who dialed the emergency number and the child who spoke to the operator had mistaken Mr. Moon's attempt to calm her for aggression. The scratches she displayed in the police photograph may have been self inflicted—from her own artificial fingernails.

As he listened to her portrayal of the seminal scene, Warren Moon sat with his head lowered. He appeared embarrassed by but not responsible for what happened. During his testimony, he similarly gave the impression of being embarrassed by, but not responsible for, what happened, as he recounted for the jury of four women and two men that on July 18, 1995, Felicia Moon had just "gone ballistic" and had to be contained. Any struggle that their son or housekeeper observed was his attempt to "calm" her. In the intensity of the courtroom and before the eagerly awaiting press, Mrs. Moon's claim that her husband had put her in fear of her life vanished, along with Mr. Moon's contrition and self-blame. She became the aggressor, and he became the victim.

The jury agreed and acquitted Warren Moon of assault charges. According to their own version of the story, the bruises and scratches Felicia Moon displayed on July 18, 1995, were typical of those you would find in any marriage. No one in the courtroom appeared more elated than she. After all, she explained, she did not want her children to think their father was "a criminal." As she exited the courtroom, she was hopeful: "My sins and my husband's sins have been forgiven. . . . We choose to go on with our marriage, with our family, and serve our Lord and Savior."

Following his acquittal, Warren and Felicia Moon appeared on the *Larry King Live* show. It was the final scene in the final act of the morality play. In their appearance, the couple talked openly about how the dual stresses of wealth and fame had strained their marriage. They spoke about how the arrest and trial had shattered what family stability they had managed to maintain. The crisis had caused each of them to reflect on what was important, to call upon their faith, and to vow to do better. Much of the public, particularly that segment who were football fans, was satisfied. Callers from the United States and Canada told Warren Moon that he was still their hero. His good-guy image was damaged but not destroyed.

Though some observers were perplexed by the shift in Felicia Moon's story, most were disappointed—not so much by the incident leading to Warren Moon's arrest as by Felicia Moon's explanation of it. How had an attempted strangulation become a family quarrel? Why would a 125-pound woman, who swiftly retreated from a fight with her 200-pound athlete husband, now swear that he was the victim? How was it that fame and success, rather than poverty and despair, resulted in a troubled marriage for the Moons? What forces might have entered into Felicia Moon's decision to ransom the privacy of their entire marriage with intimate details beyond the scope of the July 18 incident? These disappointed observers had seen in Felicia Moon an opportunity to draw public attention to the plight of abused women. But as Felicia Moon herself declared, "I'm not going to wear anybody's labels." Who could blame her? Even women who complain to the police about abuse don't want to wear a "battered woman" banner.

But to regard Felicia Moon's response as typical of any battered woman who is reluctant to testify against her husband is to ignore her reality. Mrs. Moon confessed that she believed that her husband was arrested because he is Black. In the wake of O. J. Simpson's trial for the murder of his wife, Nicole Brown Simpson—with its allegations of abuse and claims of institutionalized racism in the prosecution of Blacks—race was on everyone's minds. Even if it was not, the demonstrations outside the Texas courtroom, staged by leaders of the Black community, reminded those inside that race was indeed an issue.

To understand the conflict that both Moons felt in the face of the claim of domestic assault, one must view the allegations through the prism of this country's history of violence against women and racism in our criminal prosecutions of Black men. I am not suggesting that Mrs. Moon lied to protect her husband. I am asserting that both she and he simply shifted focus. At the trial, they steered the public and jury away from his alleged violence. She focused the story on her rage and her irrationality, much of which stemmed from the couple's troubled marriage. Both Moons knew that his celebrity status would mean that the *People v. Warren Moon*, like the Simpson trial, would become modern theater. Accepting this situation, the Moons chose to present a perspective that the jury would accept and that would save him from a hefty fine and/or imprisonment.

Felicia Moon's testimony was a clear attempt to transcend racial stereotypes about Black men even as it relied on stereotypes about irrational, emasculating Black women. Assuming that Moon was sincere, it is clear that no one factor explains the choice she made to focus only on her flaws and her failures in their marriage. Indeed, Felicia Moon did what many women do: She stood by her man. But more than devotion to Warren Moon may have led to her choice. For Felicia Moon, a whole host of factors, some that she mentioned and others that were drawn from the circumstances, might have led her to resist filing charges and testifying. Money, fame, gender, and race all entered into the equation. Few of us dared to say what we instinctively knew was the truth: Felicia Moon could easily have been driven by a desire to save the reputation of a well-known Black man not only for himself but for the entire African American community. She ultimately decided that the loss of her reputation would be less damaging to her standing in the community than would be her disloyalty to a Black male hero.

Because of the painful history of slavery and years of discrimination, the term *community* assumes a near metaphysical dimension for African Americans. We are bonded together by a history of oppression that has created in us common needs, as well as a common, though sometimes loosely defined, enemy. Stories of abuses, such as police brutality, remind us of the necessity of community and often serve as clarion calls for greater racial solidarity. Likewise, a triumph by one member of the community is seen as a victory for the entire community. Thus, stories of triumph and, ironically, stories of abuse can each be said to have some positive community value. Since athletics was historically one of the few venues in which Blacks were given an opportunity to excel, our most memorable and visible symbols of triumph are our athletes, most of whom are men. The community has developed a romance with the professional Black athlete, and like Joe Louis and Willie Mays before him, Warren Moon became the quintessential community representative. In 1989 Moon was awarded the honor of NFL Man of the Year, and during his 1991–92 season with the Houston Oilers, he was one of the highest-paid players in football. He was one of our own, and he seemed to assume the role with energy, enthusiasm, and integrity. His Crescent Moon Foundation provided scholarships for students who otherwise could not afford college and sponsored a holiday toy drive for a local hospital, and his good deeds did not end with the scholarships. He visited an orphanage while on a trip to Japan and helped serve Thanksgiving dinners at a homeless shelter. With a beautiful wife and four children, he was a family man. His picture appeared on the cover of *Ebony Man*, and the related article discussed his marriage and Felicia Moon's effort to obtain her master's degree. He was a positive "role model" and an example of the good the community had to offer.

Through his activities, Moon affirmed the African American community and thus contributed to its survival. In turn, the community supported him. In a case of her word against his or, as in the Moon case, his and her word against the White prosecutors, the community would stand by him. Even O. J. Simpson, an individual whose direct ties with the African American community were far less pronounced than Moon's, enjoyed strong community support during his trial. Moon could expect no less. Moreover, Warren Moon was a favorite of Whites as well as Blacks. When he arrived in Minnesota to play for the Vikings, the press and the fans once again lauded him as a role model. As with Simpson, popularity among Whites certainly boosted his status in the Black community. Moon might have transcended his race in popularity, but he had not forgotten it. He was one of "ours" whom "they" worshipped as well.

The adulation offered Black male athletes does not exist in a historical vacuum. It is juxtaposed daily against statistics of the unemployment rates of Black men. Indeed, the image of the Black male athlete cheered on by Whites and Blacks serves as one of the few balances against the nightly news images of handcuffed and shackled Black men being led away by largely White law enforcement officials.

Compared to what we knew of her heroic husband, the public knew little about Felicia Moon before the charge of domestic violence against her husband. During the trial, she explained why that was so. "The public doesn't know me because I don't want them to know me." Felicia Moon was beginning to understand that her concept of herself had become irrelevant, that the public had constructed its own version of her, with or without her cooperation. As the writer Zora Neale Hurston put it, "People are prone to build a statue of the kind of person that it pleases them to be." According to Warren Moon's testimony at the trial, Felicia Moon was always "feisty." Before the trial, she had been depicted in the Houston press as outspoken and frank. Though not as visible as her husband, she was an active member of a local church, a Girl Scout leader, and an administrator for the scholarship funds of the Crescent Moon Foundation. She stayed home in Texas with her children even after the Houston Oilers traded Moon to the Minnesota Vikings, a fact, she explained, that contributed to tension in the marriage. Before the trade, she responded angrily to the racist remarks that Houston fans directed at her and her children during the Oilers' losing seasons; she reportedly got into a fistfight on at least one occasion. But while every public impression she gave was that of a strong woman with her own contributions to make, in a community so ready to admire Warren Moon's athletic and community efforts and that understood the peril of being Black and male in this society, her role was clearly secondary to his. Despite her own accomplishments, she was the "good" woman behind the "great" man.

At the trial, neither her career nor her life was held in the balance, at least on the surface. His clearly were, and his were recognized to be the more important. Thus, even if she had chosen to focus her testimony on domestic violence in an attempt to win sympathetic support, in terms of community identification, Felicia Moon would always come up short next to her husband. Stories of domestic abuse are not peculiar to African Americans in general or African American women in particular, and therefore they have no positive community value as an example of African American pain or triumph. Not only would Felicia Moon's testimony about domestic violence at the hands of her husband have had no positive community value, it would have threatened the community. It would have been used by the enemy to destroy the image of one of its prized members. She lacked both the historical images of Black women being lynched and the modern-day images of Black women being wrongly accused that might have moved the community to embrace her. And without jeopardizing a Black man, she could not present a picture of a battered and beaten Black woman that might have moved the community to embrace a story of domestic violence.

Though the heightened publicity of the story of Warren and Felicia Moon increased the potential for concerns that a charge of abuse might cause harm to the community, Felicia Moon's dilemma was not unlike that of African American women whose stories are not in the news. As a consequence, the community has developed a "code of silence" where domestic violence is concerned. Joyce King, an African American woman who is the director of Renewal House, a shelter for battered women in the Boston area, is frustrated by the silence that surrounds the issue. "Those of us who want to have a dialogue about it are frozen out. When I try to talk to Black women about the problem, they tell me that we have to be careful what we say and how we say it . . . because of how Black men are treated in society." According to King, women feel they must make a choice and that "race is more important than gender." If Felicia Moon had pursued her charges of abuse, she might easily have found herself "frozen out" of the community, much like Desiree Washington, the eighteen year old who accused boxer Mike Tyson of rape. When Black ministers, the traditional community leaders, came to Tyson's defense, they did not denounce Washington directly. But in decrying racism in the arrest and prosecution of Tyson, they indirectly disparaged the value and reliability of the prosecution's chief witness, Washington, and her complicity with the racism. Few community leaders came to her defense.

Even literary references to domestic violence in Black families have been rebuffed by African Americans as harmful to the community. In her play *For Colored Girls Who Have Considered Suicide When the Rainbow Is Enuf*, Ntozake Shange's description of this and other failed aspects of Black male and female relationships met with critical acclaim but equally harsh criticism from the community. In her novel *The Color Purple*, Alice Walker wrote about the pain of incest, as well as wife beating, that the main character experienced. After the novel was filmed, Walker wrote: "The attacks, many of them personal and painful, continued for many years, right alongside the praise. . . . It was said that I hated men, black men in particular: that my ideas of equality and tolerance were harmful, even destructive to the black community." Though these responses do not reflect the sentiment of all Blacks, they are the ones that often get played out in the modern public arena where conflict is presented in particularly acerbic tones and conciliatory voices are ignored.

Despite the community-based efforts of activists like Chuck Turner of Roxbury, Massachusetts, this problem persists in the Black community, as well as in others. Turner is a counselor at Emerge, a counseling center for "men who abuse women with whom they have relationships." Now as never before, women are encouraged to file restraining orders against abusive husbands or boyfriends. In effect, restraining orders are offered as abused women's only weapon. Yet, the police cannot offer round-the-clock protection, and restraining orders are often violated. According to Turner, "one of the reasons people violate restraining orders is because they feel the community does not care."

The African American community's indifference to claims of domestic abuse does not occur in some sealed capsule where only race is a factor. It reflects the lack of concern in the larger community and survives only because domestic violence has thrived in the society at large without redress. Until recently, police dismissed incidents of wife beating as private family matters.

Women who complained had little credibility with authorities, particularly when it was their word against that of their husbands. Even if the authorities believed women when they said they were beaten, women had even less power than they do now to effect any consequence. The authorities and even family members might tell victims of abuse that their best insurance against future beatings was to keep their houses clean and their children quiet or to fix their husbands' favorite meals. Only recently, after a collective appeal from women, have police and district attorneys pursued claims of domestic abuse as criminal acts. And as the thinking goes, if the police are insensitive to the abuse of White women, they will express even less concern for claims by Black women, particularly if they already assume such behavior to be a matter of course in the Black community. Given the discouragement from all sides, then, Felicia Moon or any African American woman might well question whether pursuing a charge would ultimately benefit her.

These were the social pressures on Felicia Moon as she decided what role she would play in this complex theatrical presentation. Although the public might have assumed that her choice was between portraying Warren Moon as a hero versus a wife beater, it is perhaps more likely that Felicia Moon felt she had to choose between sticking to her story or contributing to another instance of discriminatory prosecution of a Black man. Whereas some segments viewed hers as an opportunity to become a cause célèbre in the war against domestic violence, she saw the possibility of alienating a community in which she was rooted. Though we would have liked to have seen hers as a choice between her own well-being and her husband's, she saw it as a choice between her own well-being, on the one hand, and the well-being of her husband, children, marriage, and community, on the other hand.

What Felicia Moon proved is that the choices are rarely as clear cut as the talk shows and soap operas would have the public believe. According to her own assessment, she was not the innocent victim of Warren Moon's violence. She was the difficult, demanding wife. Though the jury never said that she deserved to be bruised and battered, one juror's comment that her injuries were typical of those found in any marriage is telling. In essence, at least one juror found that she had no particular right to a marriage that was free of bruises and battering. In that context, there are perhaps many who consider hers not much of a sacrifice at all.

Many of the disappointed observers were looking for a champion for battered women—someone who would step forward in the limelight and put a celebrity's name and face to the abuse that millions of women experience in their homes. Her reputation for being "feisty" would have made Felicia Moon a great proponent of women's right to exist, free of abuse, in their intimate relationships. Certainly, the war against domestic violence deserves strong and committed proponents. But Felicia

Moon was not to become the celebrity spokesperson for such a struggle. Nowhere in her testimony did she state that she was a champion for her husband or the solidarity of the African American community. What is clear from the testimony, however, is that she was not her own champion. Given the confines of her race, gender, and place in society, being her own champion was not a choice that was offered to her. In modern morality plays, there may be no heroes, and even the most self-righteous audience feels a bit guilty in the voyeurism, but there is always room for a villain. In her testimony, Felicia Moon offered the public herself as one laden with just the right combination of negative stereotypes and common frailties to give her credibility. Perhaps this is the saddest outcome of the entire drama. For even though it may reflect some faces of Felicia Moon's experience, it does no justice to the whole. Just as tragic is the probability that it will be read as the story of all women.

Anita Faye Hill, professor of law at the University of Oklahoma College of Law, received her B.A. from Oklahoma State University in 1977 and her J.D. from Yale University Law School in 1980. Her writings include articles on bankruptcy, commercial law, civil rights, and sexual harassment. She is currently writing a memoir chronicling her experience as a witness in the 1991 confirmation hearing for Supreme Court nominee Clarence Thomas.

The Criminal Injustice System
George E. Curry

It is impossible to comprehend African Americans' attitudes toward Christopher Darden without examining the relationship between blacks and the criminal justice system, a system to which Darden was proudly and inextricably linked.

With more than 1.5 million people behind bars—one million in state and federal prisons and another half million in local jails—the United States has the highest rate of incarceration in the Western world, according to information published in 1995 by the U.S. Department of Justice's Bureau of Justice Statistics. If all these prisoners were held in one place, that place would rank as the sixth-largest city in the United States, equal to the combined populations of Cleveland, Denver, and Seattle.

Not included in that number are another 3.6 million

who are on probation or parole, meaning that 5.1 million—3 percent of the U.S. adult population—are under some form of supervision from the criminal justice system. In addition to those 5.1 million, eleven million others are booked each year in city or county jails and prisons and usually spend at least one night behind bars.

It is not surprising, then, that the United States leads the industrialized world by imprisoning 55 out of every 100,000 of its citizens, according to the Sentencing Project, a Washington-based organization that studies various aspects of the criminal justice system. The group reported that the U.S. rate is about five times that of Canada and Australia and seven times that of most European democracies.

The National Council on Crime and Delinquency in San Francisco projected that if several "get tough" measures, such as "three strikes and you're out," are implemented on a national scale, the prison population will rise to 7.5 million and annual criminal justice expenditures will skyrocket to approximately $221 billion, just $48 billion shy of the Department of Defense's 1995 budget of $269 billion.

As the United States continues to undergo what the National Criminal Justice Commission described as "the largest and most rapid expansions of a prison population in the history of the Western world," African Americans are becoming further ensnared in a criminal justice system that treats them differently from their white counterparts at every juncture—from the cop on the street deciding who gets arrested to the prosecutor deciding who gets formally charged with a crime, who gets the opportunity to plea bargain, and who serves the longest prison sentence.

"A race crisis of disastrous proportions is unfolding in the American criminal justice system," warned the National Criminal Justice Commission, a group of citizens and experts who came together to assess crime policy in America. In its report, *The Real War on Crime*, the commission stated: "A racial breakdown of the inmate population in the United States reveals that African-Americans are incarcerated at a rate more than six times that of whites—1,947 per 100,000 citizens compared to 306 per 100,000 citizens for whites. This disparity exists for two reasons: African-Americans tend to get arrested at higher rates than whites *and* they tend to be treated more harshly than whites as they move through the criminal justice system."

These figures notwithstanding, the majority of violent crimes are committed by whites. But one wouldn't be able to discern that fact from the makeup of the prison population. African American men represent less than 7 percent of the overall population in the United States, yet constitute almost half the inmates of prisons and jails.

"The difference between the numbers of minorities and whites in prison has widened as sentences for crimes have gotten longer," the National Criminal

Justice Commission's report observed. "In 1930, 75 percent of all prison admissions were white and 22 percent were African-American. That ratio has roughly reversed. In 1992, 29 percent of prison admissions were white, while 51 percent were African-American and 20 percent were Hispanic. Almost three out of four prison admissions today are either African-American or Hispanic. Ninety percent of the prison admissions for drug offenses are African-American or Hispanic."

More startling—and telling in the eyes of African Americans—is that during the height of the War on Drugs in 1989, blacks were arrested on drug charges at a rate five times that of whites, even though federal statistics showed that blacks and whites were abusing drugs at about the same rate. What further ensures that the rate of incarceration among African Americans will be higher than among whites is that the legal penalties for crack cocaine, which is most likely to be used by African Americans, are up to one hundred times harsher than the penalties for powder cocaine, the drug of choice among whites.

Another revealing figure highlights the contrast between wrongdoers in the streets and criminals in executive suites. According to the Justice Department, losses from all personal and household crimes totaled approximately $19.1 billion in 1991. In the same year, white-collar crimes, such as the savings-and-loan scandal, amounted to between $130 billion and $472 billion—seven to twenty times as much as for street crime. Yet, it is often the lowly street peddler who is prosecuted to the full extent the law allows, while the corporate criminal receives only minimal punishment, if any.

Given this record, which was abbreviated here for the sake of space, African Americans had more than ample reason to be suspicious of the criminal justice system as O. J. Simpson went on trial for murder. It was not that O. J. loomed large as an endearing figure among blacks— the *Pittsburgh Courier* sardonically noted that even his Ford Bronco was white—it was that African Americans continue to view the criminal justice system as a criminal injustice system.

Even Darden's father immediately recognized the danger of his son helping to prosecute Simpson in such a racially charged atmosphere. "You'll catch hell if you work on that one," the elder Darden predicted. But Christopher thought otherwise. In his book, *In Contempt*, written with Jess Walter, Darden recalled: "I had naively believed my presence would, in some way, embolden my black brothers and sisters, show them that this was their system as well, that we were making *progress*." For his naïveté, Darden wrote, "I was branded an Uncle Tom, a traitor used by The Man."

From the start, though, it was clear that race was going to be an overwhelming issue in the Simpson trial; Darden's presence only magnified the complexity. When the trial began, this country's racial divide could be illustrated by any number of rich examples. Deval

Patrick, assistant U.S. attorney general for civil rights in the first Clinton administration, offered a short list of names and places that symbolize America's racial problem: Forsyth County, Georgia; Willie Horton; Charles Stuart; Susan Smith; Rodney King; South Central Los Angeles; Randolph County, Alabama; and Denny's. He could have added Texaco; Avis; St. Petersburg, Florida; and Jonny Gammage. Perhaps the most potent example was the case of Rodney King, which lurked in the background as Simpson's trial got under way. Although the two cases had little in common, no one could forget the videotape of an unarmed King being brutally beaten by Los Angeles cops. And it was difficult for people of color to have faith in a criminal justice system that acquitted the white policemen—though they were convicted at a second trial—in the face of such overwhelming evidence captured on videotape.

In the midst of this racially charged atmosphere of distrust and suspicion, the prosecution added Darden to their team after the jury had been selected. Darden's belated addition to the prosecution team raised cries of window dressing, a criticism that stung the forever-brooding Darden.

It didn't help that Johnnie Cochran, referring to Darden, told reporters, "All of a sudden, he shows up here. Now why is that, after we have eight African Americans [on the jury]? Why now?"

Darden wrote, "Now he was accusing me of being a sellout. I understand that he had a job to do, to protect his client. But this had nothing to do with that. This was a private message. . . . Blacks could hear what he was saying between the lines: *This brother is being used by the Man. This brother is an Uncle Tom.* It was the most offensive thing a black could be called by another black, and hearing it repeated on television and in the newspapers was the equivalent of publicly being called a nigger by a white lawyer."

Darden, justifiably upset over the name-calling and eager to defend his role in prosecuting Simpson, spent much of his book denigrating the jury, which, he said, "picked a dreadful time to seek an empty retribution for Rodney King and a meaningless payback for a system of bigotry, segregation and slavery." Almost lost in Darden's account of the Simpson trial is that African Americans have strong feelings about crime, which ravages their communities, and as jurors, do not hesitate to convict African Americans every day throughout the United States. Many, if not most, African Americans have a sense of fair play and require, like all citizens, that prosecutors *prove* their cases before convicting suspects. Evidently, the jurors were not persuaded by the evidence and testimony assembled by Marcia Clark, Darden, and other members of their team.

After the jury rendered its verdict, America was divided again, with many—though not all—African Americans believing that the case against Simpson had not been proved and many whites reaching the opposite conclusion. It was shocking proof for many of the true wideness of the rift between black and white Americans, a rift that many had hoped was narrowing. As New Jersey Senator Bill Bradley said in a 1996 speech in Los Angeles, "Slavery was America's original sin, and race remains its unresolved dilemma." Clearly, that unresolved dilemma remains just that—unresolved. Ask any African American, even one who is said to have "made it," and he or she will recount incident after incident of racism, personal slights, and double standards that ensure ongoing feelings of alienation from white Americans.

If most Americans will gain some personal experience of the criminal justice system at one point or another— from which they will draw personal conclusions about its fairness or unfairness—perhaps even more powerful than these personal perceptions are the images transmitted by the mass media. The media circus of the Simpson trial is only one example of the myriad ways in which the mass media influence public opinion—most examples are less obvious and certainly more insidious. Reflecting on more than a quarter of a century in the print media—the first twenty-three years in the so-called mainstream press and the last four as editor-in-chief of *Emerge: Black America's Newsmagazine*—I have come to the inescapable conclusion that most major newspapers, magazines, and broadcast outlets never routinely show African Americans in their full diversity, the good along with the bad. Although many of the major news organizations are well intentioned, or at least pretend to be, they portray Black America as some kind of freak show, replete with welfare queens, fatherless families, drug kingpins, and others who couldn't spell the letter "a." To make sure that no one accuses them of racism, they throw in stories on black athletes and entertainers, many of whom are estranged from their communities, for good measure.

The white media (and make no mistake, the media *are* white) have an image problem—not their own image, but the image they choose to portray of people of color and women in their normal course of business. All too often, African Americans are interviewed only if the stories are about race and women, if the issue is abortion or the gender gap in politics. It has always amazed me that local television reporters across the country perform the same feat independently of one another: They appear at a crime scene and manage to find the one black male witness who sports a gold tooth (only one, if we're lucky) and a plastic bag on his head. Moreover, this eyewitness typically makes African American viewers cringe with each ungrammatical utterance. I'm not suggesting that journalists should not interview such characters, but I do find it suspicious that these episodes are repeated with such frequency, given what I know of the diversity of the African American community.

There are some examples of the networks performing as they should. In particular, I remember one report on *CBS News with Dan Rather* about then-president

Ronald Reagan's health; I was stunned to see a black physician being interviewed. The fact that he was affiliated with Howard University, a historically black institution in Washington, D.C., made this interview especially memorable. Perhaps more telling than its occurrence, though, is the fact that I remember it; if the incident was in any way routine, I doubt I would, now more than a decade after it was reported.

The issue of how people are perceived—by others as well as themselves—is a critical one, and nowhere more critical than it is for African Americans. In fact, it is now commonplace that if a group wants to put a national issue, such as welfare or affirmative action, in a negative light, the first step is to connect the issue to a black face, however skewed the perception it may create that blacks are the majority of those who are incarcerated, on welfare, or benefit from affirmative action. George Bush's use of black convict Willie Horton in the 1988 presidential campaign is a classic example. Rather than allowing themselves to be co-opted in such schemes, in effect, rendering themselves the tools of orchestrated campaigns designed to sway public opinion, journalists have an obligation to judge and present the issues on the basis of their merits, not according to their sensationalism.

One way of getting beyond the propaganda is to reexamine how journalists cover the news. Considering that the welfare rolls are about evenly divided between whites and blacks, that reality is not portrayed on television. Whether it's welfare or crime, the face you're most likely to see on the television screen is that of an African American.

But moving beyond the stereotypes requires sensitivity. During the 1988 campaign, I, as a Washington correspondent for the *Chicago Tribune*, was assigned to interview an inner-city welfare recipient and a suburban voter on issues they thought were important to them. I did exactly as I was told: I found a white woman on welfare in the District of Columbia and an African American living in a Virginia suburb. The bureau's news editor at the time, Randolph Murray, a white Southerner, applauded my taking that extra step.

On another occasion, I wrote and served as chief correspondent for "The Assault on Affirmative Action," which was aired as part of the *Frontline* series on the Public Broadcasting System. Scott Craig, an independent producer in Chicago with whom I was working, and I decided to move beyond the well-established stereotypes. So we taped a white Republican, Mayor William Hudnut of Indianapolis, arguing for affirmative action and Walter Williams, a black economist, arguing against it. I don't know how many viewers tried to adjust the color on their television sets, but I thought we had given people another way of viewing the world.

Presenting stereotypical images is not the only shortcoming of the so-called mainstream media. Another problem is how the media present information. Allegations of a liberal bias are frequently trumpeted by conservative groups. But if there is a bias in the media—and I contend that there is, however unintentional—it is against people of color, the poor, and women. Moreover, when issues that are important to African Americans are presented, they are done in a fashion that is either incomplete or flawed.

The issue of affirmative action is a good example. Sophisticated right-wing groups have learned that to defeat a candidate or program, it is necessary to tar the object with a label. In the case of affirmative action, which is essentially a conservative remedy that gained popularity under Richard Nixon, a Republican, it has to be linked to bogeymen by such terms as *quotas* or *preferential treatment.*

In news stories, critics are allowed to toss around the term *quotas* in reference to affirmative action with no challenging word from reporters, even though Executive Order 11246, the presidential order that created affirmative action, states: "Goals may not be rigid and inflexible quotas which must be met, but must be targets reasonably attainable by means of applying every good faith effort to make all aspects of the entire affirmative action program work." The word *preferences* is another that is used to inflame passion and to create confusion. As Patrick, former assistant attorney general for civil rights, explained: "We are said to receive undeserved special privileges, while we know that hardly a single white would willingly trade places with us today."

Still, the white media have adopted the anti-affirmative-action language of conservatives and, in the process, misframed the issue. In 1995, for example, the *Washington Post* reported that most Americans were opposed to affirmative action. Its conclusion was based on a biased and poorly worded question: whether the respondents thought "women, blacks and other minorities should receive preference in hiring, promotions and college admissions to make up for past discrimination." By using the term *preference*, the newspaper predetermined the outcome. However, as polls conducted by such newspapers as the *Wall Street Journal*, *USA Today*, and the *Los Angeles Times* and other media organizations have found, when the question is phrased in a more even-handed manner, such as, "Do you support affirmative action programs as long as they do not use quotas and as long as the individuals involved are qualified?" a solid majority of Americans support affirmative action.

Pollster Lou Harris, writing in *The Affirmative Action Debate*, an anthology I edited in 1996, observed: "Sadly, the media, including many of the most respected newspapers, have done the public a disservice by continually referring to 'preferential treatment' or 'preferences' or 'racial preference programs' as interchangeable with affirmative action. Of course, under the *Bakke* and *Weber* Supreme Court decisions in the late 1970s, quotas were outlawed and have been illegal ever since." Moreover, by using *preferences* interchangeably with *affirmative action*, some journalists have erroneously concluded that support for affirmative action has eroded. As Harris noted, "*U.S. News and World Report*, in an article by Steven Roberts, dedicated almost an entire issue to proclaiming the demise of public support for affirmative action. The polling data cited in the article draw mainly on polls that asked about 'preferential treatment.' . . . Such reporting has contributed in a major way toward the confusion over the real state of public opinion on affirmative action. And that confusion has political consequences."

Meanwhile, the covers of the newsweeklies are just as telling as the slant of the articles inside. The cover of *U.S. News and World Report* featured a facsimile of a classified ad and the words, "Does Affirmative Action Mean: No White Men Need Apply?" *Newsweek*'s cover, featuring a white fist and a black fist, was no better, with its headline trumpeting "Race and Rage: When Preferences Work—and Don't." In contrast, the cover of *Emerge* magazine had an image of a shade being let down on the face of an African American, with the question, "Colorblind or Racist?" and contained no mention of that dangerously misunderstood word *preferences*. Because many print journalists double as media pundits, the flaws in their writing are transferred to television and radio programs. Martin Luther King Jr. often referred to 11 A.M. Sunday as the most segregated hour in America, when African Americans and whites worship in separate churches. Now, almost thirty years after his assassination, this hour on Sunday morning is still the most segregated in the nation—especially if one is watching one of the national roundtable discussions among journalists. Except for Black Entertainment Television's *Lead Story*, which features African American journalists, most of these programs include only white journalists. The fact that these journalists can freely discuss people of color, civil rights issues, and the O. J Simpson case without questioning the makeup of their panels is testament to their arrogance.

In the eyes of most African Americans, the Simpson case—and Darden's role in it—was as much about America's criminal justice system and how the case was portrayed in the media as it was about whether the former football star had murdered two innocent victims. And as long as race remains America's unresolved dilemma, infiltrating so many areas of everyday life, it will be difficult, though not impossible, to focus solely on the merits of many issues. Clearly, African Americans have been given no reason to trust the criminal justice system or the mainstream media that report it. In distinctly different ways, each has failed to provide a fundamental expectation of American society—basic fairness.

George E. Curry is editor-in-chief of Emerge: Black America's Newsmagazine, *based in Washington, D.C. He has been a reporter for* Sports Illustrated *and the* St. Louis Post-Dispatch *and a Washington correspondent and New York bureau chief for the* Chicago Tribune. *Curry is the editor of the essay collection* The Affirmative Action Debate *(published by Addison-Wesley) and has appeared on many national television programs, including* CBS News with Dan Rather, World News Tonight with Peter Jennings, *the* Today *show,* Good Morning America, *and* Nightline.

The Changing Climate and the Challenge Ahead
—— WADE HENDERSON

The O. J. Simpson saga was a multidimensional tragedy. Beyond the pain of the crime and its aftermath, the trial was an intensely theatrical morality play. The entire affair was opera come to life. In the end, justice in action is not necessarily a pretty sight, but like it or not, the system worked. And despite the many lapses into absurdity, the Simpson saga, in all its dimensions, did say something important about race relations in America. It told us how deep the divide in racial attitudes in the United States remains, it highlighted the tortured path African Americans negotiate on the frontiers of American race relations, and it illuminated deep fissures in the American criminal justice system.

BOLD, BLACK, AND BEAUTIFUL

Many observers were uncomfortable with the racial dimensions of the Simpson story. But even when race was not mentioned directly or openly, issues of race were often the unspoken subtext of the saga, and race played an important role in every aspect of the proceedings. Even if one could have begun watching the trial denying the importance of race, the discovery of the tapes of Mark Fuhrman, Fuhrman's admission that he used the "N" word over and over, and references to "playing the race card" throughout the trial put any such doubts to rest. Moreover, the fact that Simpson's interracial marriage would have been illegal throughout the United States less than thirty years ago was itself an illustration of the remarkable evolution of American laws and values over the past forty years.

Just two generations ago, a black man who was accused of Simpson's crime would have been lucky to survive the trial, much less to be acquitted by a "jury of his peers" for killing a white woman, at least in the South. As a matter of fact, since African Americans were systematically barred from jury service, Simpson could not even have been tried by a jury of his peers, his wealth notwithstanding.

And yet, here was America in the late 1990s, in the midst of a horrific murder trial, quietly celebrating how far the nation has progressed in racial terms. For example, *Jet Magazine*, the social bible of Black America, ran, as one of its Week's Best Photos, a provocative shot called "Celebrity Prosecutors," which described Christopher Darden and Marcia Clark as among the notables on hand for the 1995 Noel Foundation Awards Dinner at the Beverly Hilton Hotel. Somehow, it would be hard to imagine this all-too-friendly pose by members of almost any other team of prosecutors in any other murder trial; in the case of the Simpson trial, though, it seemed almost right. Prosecutorial chic.

Thus, the Simpson trial gave the world a romanticized and distorted view of the criminal justice system and of racial interaction in America—and not merely because of its celebrity defendant.

Television created powerful and lasting images at the Simpson trial. The nation was riveted. Physical appearance mattered. Everyone involved was beautiful—O. J., the late Nicole Brown Simpson and Ronald Goldman, the lawyers—even Marcia Clark had a makeover during the trial in recognition of the power of the public image. Except for the ill-fitting glove incident, for the most part the lawyers projected competence and exuded the confident charm we associate with the American Dream of success.

CNN and the other news media made Johnnie Cochran an international star, particularly among African Americans and in the Third World. Cochran's eloquence and tactical brilliance left the prosecution flat. Darden, on the other hand, and in spite of defeat, became a sympathetic symbol, as a black man willing to defend with personal integrity the judicial system of American values, even in the face of growing skepticism about the integrity of the proceedings, not to mention accusations of police misconduct and prosecutorial collusion.

The images of the Simpson trial were strangely comforting to the nation. As with many African Americans, I took personal satisfaction in seeing fellow black people and other people of color serving as major players—as trial attorneys, judge, jurors, forensic experts, detectives, and pundits—throughout the trial. I am old enough to remember the period in recent history when such accomplishments were rare. The mere presence of Judge Lance Ito, Clark, Darden, and Cochran in the same trial in their respective roles, for example, must have been a "first" of sorts. The images of these highly competent professionals of various hues said much to a nation in need of good news on racial progress.

Less than fifty years ago, the meaningful practice of law was virtually off-limits to women, blacks, and Asian Americans. Both Clark and Darden are clearly qualified, and it is likely that they benefited from affirmative action programs of recruitment and outreach. Moreover, fifty years ago, Judge Ito could not have served on the bench; instead, he would have been incarcerated as a domestic detainee of war in a camp for Japanese Americans. Today, his service on the bench not only reflects his ability as a jurist, but involves considerations regarding the importance of diversity in the criminal justice system.

Perception is everything in both politics and life. In the eyes of opponents of affirmative action, the nation has advanced so far that assistance to stop present-day discrimination is unnecessary and turns equality on its head. If one was interested in supporting that argument, one would have to look no further than the racially mixed prosecution and defense teams who sat beside each other in the courtroom. To those same minds, perhaps Senator Alphonse D'Amato's joke on *The Bob Grant Show* about Judge Ito's mannerisms had nothing to do with Ito's Asian ancestry. Perhaps no one even noticed that Cochran and Darden were black.

But of course D'Amato's joke was offensive to many, and the color of Darden and Cochran's skins is a fact that escaped no one. And it would be too easy—and wrong—to project from Simpson's acquittal that America has achieved, at least in part, the ideal of *E Pluribus Unum*—"out of many, one." As a nation we know that progress toward ending racial discrimination under the law has been more readily achieved over the past thirty years than progress toward ending racial bias in reality. But even that assumption is perhaps too optimistic when one considers that as we celebrate the achievements of the Civil Rights Act of 1964 or the Voting Rights Act of 1965, the meaningful implementation of these laws faces renewed assault. Racism, bigotry, and intolerance are ingrained in the American soil. The U.S. Commission on Civil Rights reported in 1995 that the enforcement of federal and state civil rights laws is woefully underfunded across the board. Without attention, the problem is growing like weeds. The recent wave of arson at African American churches in the Southeast, as well as increased hate crimes against Asian Americans and Hispanic Americans, gays and lesbians, and women is evidence of the problem.

Discrimination in the criminal justice system is even more profoundly damaging and is largely ignored. Ironically, just a few doors away from Judge Ito's courtroom, and in courtrooms like his all across the nation, African American and Hispanic American men are being hustled off to federal and state prisons by the thousands, doing time as casualties of the War on Drugs. In the wake of the Simpson verdict, the Fuhrman tapes, and a recent report that almost one in three young black men is under court or prison supervision, one may hope that the nation would yet again focus its attention on racial inequalities in the criminal justice system.

One feels little hope that such a focus will come from the government, however. Political indifference to racial problems is institutionalized and bipartisan in America. The massive profits flowing from the prison-industry complex—the new economic engine of depressed communities—further discourage real progress. Perhaps the most egregious example of the endless resources the government is willing to invest in building prisons, as opposed to keeping people out of prison, can be found in the rejection by Congress and President Clinton in

1996 of a change in federal policy on sentences for the possession and sale of cocaine. Currently, the law draws a major distinction between penalties for the possession and sale of "crack" and "powder" cocaine. Although the effect of both drugs is similar, the federal law dictates that sentences for the use or sale of crack cocaine are one hundred times greater than sentences involving the same amount of powder cocaine. Not coincidentally, crack is used mostly by inner-city blacks and powder cocaine mostly by suburban whites. Congress brazenly thumbed its nose at the experts it appointed to study and advise it on establishing a policy on cocaine and chose to punish equal crimes differently. The result is that black offenders are typically sentenced to five years in prison and white offenders typically receive probation for committing the same crime. Of the more than five hundred recommendations submitted by the Sentencing Commission, this was the first one Congress rejected.

Few issues more graphically demonstrate race-based disparities in the criminal justice system than the policy on cocaine. Such gross unfairness is made all the more tragic by its cynicism. The absence of fairness breeds contempt for the law and racial polarization. To his credit, President Clinton has been willing to speak out on racial differences that confront the nation. On the day of the Million Man March, for example, in one of his best speeches on the subject of race, Clinton acknowledged that "African Americans have lived too long with a justice system that in too many cases has been, and continues to be, less than just." He also acknowledged the disproportionate rate of incarceration of blacks.

However, by rejecting the Sentencing Commission's recommendation, President Clinton missed an important opportunity to bridge the nation's racial divide. His support of Congress's racially divisive action will only perpetuate discrimination in the criminal justice system. Among the most vocal opponents of changing the federal law were several members of the House of Representatives who strongly supported the formation of a presidential commission on racial problems. But when such a commission spoke out on racial equality in the criminal justice system, they fell by the wayside in a cynical bow to politics.

THE SHIFTING PARADIGM

The racial divide and the dilemma African Americans face were exacerbated by the Republican landslide in the November 1994 elections. It is too early to predict a "watershed" change in the electorate; however, the dramatic shift in Congress and in many state legislatures toward the ideological Right is readily apparent. The new Congress, at least the House, only partially implemented its promise for the Contract with America, but themes of "defunding the Left" (refusing to appropriate funds for programs, such as the National Endowment for the Arts and Humanities and the Legal Services Corporation), that the right wing considered left wing and a return to "states' rights"—the devolution of federal power—run silently through much of the work of the 104th Congress. Legislation to block "unfunded mandates" passed easily; the attempt to abolish the Legal Services Corporation, with its emphasis on aiding the poor, failed, but the program was severely weakened. Whatever else happened, though—whatever the political or ideological explanation of the event—a massive power shift occurred from the Democratic Party to the Republican Party, from an ill-defined liberalism to a main street conservatism, that ushered in a highly restrictive view of the government's role in American society.

The real prize—the crown jewel—of the Republican Revolution of the 104th Congress was welfare reform. Welfare reform achieved everything the new leaders said they wanted: It broke the sixty-year-old federal entitlement to assistance in time of need; restored states' rights by setting up federal block grants under the control of the states; squeezed $56 billion dollars from an already shortchanged system, which means that tax cuts for upper-income persons are now a realistic possibility; and shifted the public debate away from poverty to a concern for the moral values of recipients, even though the bill reportedly includes $12 billion less than what is needed for jobs.

The fact that these savings come on the backs of children, legal immigrants, and poor people is, of course, directly related to the fact that these groups do not vote. The fact that President Clinton would sign such a bill, thereby repealing the New Deal social safety net of Franklin D. Roosevelt, is by far the bigger issue and represents the birth of the New Democrat.

Many progressive forces, among African Americans and other groups, are wondering what it all means. How should they respond to the new political realities? After all, this is the first time in forty years that Republicans have driven the agenda in both houses of Congress, leaving civil rights organizations to work in an unfamiliar world.

Simple pragmatism suggests that African Americans should reach out to the new Republican leaders. But with the notable exception of Jack Kemp, who "flip-flopped" on affirmative action less than two days after being selected as Dole's running mate, the jury is still out on which of its two faces the Republican Party presents. As the "Party of Lincoln," Republicans are rightly proud of a history of breaking down barriers of discrimination and promoting equal opportunity. But the Republican Party is also the one that conceived of President Nixon's racially targeted "Southern strategy," which painted Democrats as the party of racial minorities, unions, and the poor.

Racial and social antagonisms in the 1994 elections were exhibited in two ways: as a Southern white-male backlash against Clinton's policies in support of gays in the military and gun control and as the racially coded manipulation of the debates on welfare and crime.

Tragically, while Republicans were ready to tar the Democrats as soft on special interests (such as African Americans), the Democrats were all too ready to agree with them and to blame their most loyal supporters for their problems getting elected. As usual, black voters in 1994 were especially loyal to the Democrats, giving Democratic candidates 88 percent of their votes. But facts never get in the way of a good theory. Despite their overwhelming support, many Democrats blamed the creation of black-majority congressional districts in Southern states under the Voting Rights Act for making it harder for Democrats to win in other districts. They argued that concentrating black voters in districts for the purpose of electing black congresspersons denied white Democrats crucial (loyal) support from black voters.

Unfortunately for African Americans, the post-'94 debate among Democrats has been dominated by the party's more conservative voices. Among the more respected voices is the Democratic Leadership Council (DLC), the "centrist" Democratic political wing of the party that President Clinton and Vice President Al Gore helped to found. The members of this council often speak in political code, but certainly none was needed here. "If the 1994 midterm election signaled anything, it was the death of the New Deal political alignment and the programmatic approaches it spawned," wrote Al From, president of the DLC, in *The New Democrat*.

Racial code words were especially evident in the congressional debate over welfare reform. In spite of the intensity of the debate over costs, welfare reform is really not about money. Aid to Families with Dependent Children (AFDC) costs only about 1 percent of the national budget, and meaningful welfare reform would actually be more costly than the present system. Rather, the debate was about something much more important—breaking the entitlement status of welfare and how and for whom the money is to be used.

Welfare reform was also about winning elections. According to most accounts and many White House insiders, the president overruled the suggestion of his chief of staff and secretary of health and human services not to sign the welfare bill on the recommendation of the White House Rasputin who engineered his post-'94 political comeback. Jonathan Alter reported in the *Washington Post* that President Clinton's political guru, Dick Morris, did not attend the two-and-a-half-hour cabinet meeting on welfare reform at which the president decided to sign the bill. However, Morris reportedly kept track by telephone, and when he heard the decision, he "exulted to a friend, 'That's it. The election is over.'" The friend added, "Morris is famous for his melodramatics, but his instincts may have been right."

THE WELFARE METAPHOR

How did this country come to the point of repealing welfare, and what does the repeal have to do with America's racial divide? There is little doubt that the bill that became law is harsh and punitive. Could it have been different? Perhaps, but at Union Station in Washington one day, I saw just how far to the right the fear and loathing of poor blacks has moved.

I noticed the photograph of the young woman and her baby on the cover of the magazine the moment I walked up to the newsstand. It would have been hard to miss it. The portrait, artfully displayed on a red-orange background, seemed to jump off the magazine rack. I did not know this young woman, but as strange as it may seem, I did recognize her. What made her familiar to me was the context in which the photograph appeared, as well as the magazine's "artistic sensibility." Who among us would say that the photograph was not beautifully executed? After all, it was appearing on the cover of the *New Republic*, one of the nation's most respected publications. And one might argue that the artistic arrangement (whether natural or staged) of the mother and child in muted tones of brown against the red-orange background had an almost sympathetic quality.

But there was also an unsettling tension in the photograph and in the cover presentation. The editors designed a provocative, bold layout. This special issue of the magazine was about welfare in America—and who gets it—and obviously, since it was appearing in the *New Republic*, I assumed that it had something to say. The initial impression of sympathy gained from the tranquillity of the photograph was clearly false, and in the end, I felt betrayed by the magazine's intellectual dishonesty.

The *New Republic* has influence. As a well-regarded voice of political opinion, its recommendations and images speak volumes to political leaders and the public. Certainly, I was angry that the editors had endorsed the welfare reform bill that I believe will be harmful to a substantial number of poor women and children. But I was also angry at the way the issues were presented by the magazine and what was said to justify the endorsement.

Perhaps I was angry, at least in part, because of the banner headline over the woman's head that screamed, "DAY OF RECKONING," with its biblical implications—a harsh admonition to those undeserving poor women who fail to repent their sins.

Perhaps I burned because of what my heightened awareness told me is stereotyping—the subtle but effective manipulation of a powerful poignant photographic image to make a distorted and unsavory point. Of course, I noticed immediately that the woman in the photograph was African American. I realized that according to the actual number of welfare recipients, she could just as easily have been white, but in the context of the Great Welfare Debate of '96, this young African American woman was transmogrified into Welfare Mother, the enemy.

As portrayed in the photograph, this young woman is the embodiment of all that is wrong with the welfare system. For example, one assumes that she is the mother of the infant. There is a curler in her hair, yet she is fully dressed. She is smoking a cigarette next to her feeding baby. She is young; she could easily be a teenager. By definition, she is unmarried. One could infer any number of other troubling scenarios; for example, she is either a mother lounging inappropriately at home, rather than working, or equally disturbing, she is inappropriately dressed for an appointment. Her appearance conveys indifference. No matter what one infers, however, she is by no means a sympathetic figure. In fact, she is no longer a person. She has become one of the social entitlements that, at the end of the twentieth century, we have come to resent because of their ever-present need and their persistence in remaining among us. Bob Herbert, a columnist for the *New York Times*, put it this way: "Troubled times require the comforting presence of scapegoats . . . and welfare recipients have become the official national scapegoats."

The caption under the *New Republic* cover photograph read, "Sign the Welfare Bill Now—the Editors." Inside the magazine, the editors made this point:

> We supported Clinton's [welfare] plan and hoped he would pass it before pursuing his ambitious health care reform. He didn't. We wish it were the bill he is now being asked to sign. It isn't. Instead, a Republican Congress is sending him a bill that replaces AFDC with "block grants" for states to spend on aid programs of their own devising. Readers of responsible editorial

pages know by now that this block grant approach is "dead wrong" (*Washington Post*), even "an obscene act of social regression" (Senator Daniel Patrick Moynihan, quoted approvingly by *The New York Times*). Several of our own contributors this week agree.

So why should Clinton sign it? Not because all the liberal complaints are unjustified. The bill is, as of this writing, a nasty piece of work in many respects—made nastier by the cynical desire of some Republicans to bait Clinton into a politically damaging veto. But it has one virtue that overrides its flaws; it will, finally, start the process by which America's underclass problem can be solved.

At the heart of this editorial is the inherent, and knowingly false, assumption that there are enough jobs for those who want to work. Without adequate jobs, the revised welfare program is a cruel hoax, whose innocent victims will be children.

The assumption that jobs that provide living wages are readily available has been shared by political campaigns since the 1980s, when the image of the typical welfare recipient was made famous by then-former-Governor Ronald Reagan as the undeserving "welfare queen," the woman who is capable of working but who abuses the welfare system illegitimately. The inference is that these women are largely inner-city, substance-abusing blacks and Hispanics who spawn intergenerational poverty and an ever-growing underclass.

Of course, the truth is that only 38 percent of the AFDC recipients are black, roughly the same proportion as the percentage of white recipients. About 72 percent of all recipients have only one or two children, and only about 8 percent are under age twenty, according to Mark Greenberg, an expert on welfare reform at the Center for Law and Public Policy in Washington. Moreover, most experts agree that poverty and the lack of jobs are the real problems with welfare reform, not laziness or any of the other offensive words used to describe welfare recipients. Joel Handler, a professor of law at the University of California, Los Angeles, who has studied the welfare system for decades, noted that thirty-five million Americans live below the poverty line of $11,890 for a family of three. But the facts of welfare and poverty in this country remain ignored, and in the public mind, as on the cover of the *New Republic*, the welfare debate will remain a thinly veiled attack on poor, black women and "welfare queens."

WHERE ARE WE GOING?

Where is the nation headed on the unresolved questions of race? We are only a few years from the start of the next century, yet the social and political demons of a bygone era—and their present-day mutations—continue to haunt the progress of African Americans. Certainly, W. E. B. DuBois was correct when he observed that the problem of the twentieth century would be the problem of the "color line." But even DuBois would have been surprised by the present state of Black America in both its progress and its failure.

Some African Americans, like Simpson at the beginning of his trial and Darden by the end, might seem to have it made. Both Simpson and Darden are affluent by middle-class standards (with additional potential wealth from book deals), and by virtue of their celebrity, they had "crossed over" to become icons of white America. At the same time, however, it is also clear that the dream of equal opportunity is fading fast for many young African Americans and an increasing number of poor people across the country. This is the case notwithstanding favorable local economic conditions in many cities and strong black political leadership. In fact, as Gary Orfield and Carole Ashkenaze wrote in *The Closing Door: Conservative Policy and Black Opportunity*, many of the basic elements of the American Dream—a good job, a decent income, a house, college education for the children—are less accessible for young Americans today than they were in the mid-1970s.

Indeed, the modern civil rights movement has been highly successful in moving the United States toward becoming the more perfect Union of its constitutional promise. Through direct social action, legislation, and precedent-setting litigation, the web of legal and political sinews that gave flesh to America's unique form of apartheid was destroyed.

Despite these accomplishments, however, the birthright promise of America (as in the words of Langston Hughes, "O, let America be America again/The land that never has been yet/and yet must be . . . ") has never been truly fulfilled for African Americans.

Certainly, progress is undeniable. However, all African Americans face discrimination; and in some respects, African Americans in the inner city face it poorer, less well educated, and arguably more hopeless than when Martin Luther King Jr. gave his life for the future of the nation in 1968. Today, for example, some forty-two years after *Brown v. Board of Education*, public education remains largely segregated along both racial and economic lines, and the present Supreme Court has imposed what may be terminal restrictions on *Brown*'s continued viability. The Court's 1995 decision in *Missouri v. Jenkins* constrains federal courts from imposing effective remedies to achieve equal educational opportunity. Specifically, it prohibited a federal judge, even in a community with a history of racial discrimination and resistance to change, from imposing a community-wide tax that would be used to fund qualitative educational improvements and efforts to desegregate schools.

Moreover, public attitudes toward the resolution of the continuing problems of African Americans and the poor have hardened. This hardening was certainly evident in the public debate over welfare, but it can also be seen in public discussions about taxes, Medicare, and social security. One of President Reagan's indirect legacies is the high budgetary deficits he fostered that all but preclude the use of federal funds to promote meaningful social change. Confronting the chilling legacy of these deficits is the first element of the shifting paradigm on civil rights.

Indeed, African Americans have been buffeted over the past several years by a series of adverse Supreme Court decisions on affirmative action in contracting and education, particularly *Croson v. City of Richmond* (1989) and *Adarand Constructor, Inc. v. Pena* (1995). Together these decisions raised the legal barrier that must be overcome to justify affirmative action programs for minority businesses.

The ripple effects of the decisions have had consequences for minority businesses at all levels. In federal procurement, for example, $1 billion in minority contracts through the Department of Defense were frozen in 1996. Decisions such as this have also brought chaos to the question of how the nation is to create meaningful equal opportunities in education, employment, and contracting in the face of attacks by the conservative Court.

The Federal Court of Appeals' decision in *Hopwood v. Texas*, which set aside a race-based admissions program at the University of Texas School of Law, nullified (at least in the Fifth Circuit—Texas, Louisiana, and Mississippi) the Supreme Court's controlling decision in *Bakke v. University of California*. In *Podberesky v. Kirwan*, the Fourth Circuit Court of Appeals (Maryland, Virginia, North Carolina, and West Virginia) killed the Benjamin Banneker scholarship program for high-achieving minority students. Together, these decisions have shaken

American institutions of higher education at a time when their affirmative action programs seemed to be working.

In effect, the conservative majority of Supreme Court justices have rewritten the legal doctrines interpreting equal opportunity in the face of ongoing societal discrimination. They did so in a series of largely 5-to-4 decisions, with Justice Clarence Thomas, only the second African American to serve on the Court, writing for the majority.

President George Bush's cynical appointment of Justice Thomas, who apparently has no Darden Dilemma, to the Supreme Court was met with consternation, anger, and confusion in the African American community. African Americans wanted another African American voice to replace the strength of principle of their beloved Justice Thurgood Marshall. However, a perverse manipulation of that sentiment brought someone to the Court who was Marshall's antithesis. Organizations including the National Association for the Advancement of Colored People, the NAACP Legal Defense and Educational Fund, and the Congressional Black Caucus can take solace from their opposition to Thomas, but in the end, the confirmation of his appointment to the Court was a blow. His appointment solidified a conservative majority on the Court. It represents the second tremor of the shifting civil rights paradigm.

Republican leaders in the House made the abolition of affirmative action an unwritten provision of the Contract with America, hoping that affirmative action would become a "wedge issue" in the 1996 campaign. Taking their cue from Congress, opponents of affirmative action in several states filed voter initiatives seeking to repeal affirmative action programs. The Supreme Court's decision in *Adarand* added fuel to the fire by making it significantly more difficult to justify federal race-based affirmative action programs. Under *Adarand*, a federal affirmative action program will be subjected to "strict scrutiny" by the court. It will remain constitutional only if it is narrowly tailored and can be shown to accomplish a compelling governmental interest, such as remedying discrimination. Republicans who were vying to be presidential candidates in the 1996 campaign tripped over themselves to see who could oppose the affirmative action policy more strongly, even though several had previously supported it. The eventual Republican nominee, Senator Bob Dole, was the putative winner in the contest among his colleagues by becoming the original sponsor of legislation to repeal federal affirmative action programs.

Only a few years before, Dole was the sponsor of the federal Glass Ceiling Commission, which was created in the mid-1980s to assess the continuing need for affirmative action in private industry for women and people of color. A recent report from the commission showed that white men still retained about 95 percent of senior management positions, notwithstanding the presence of affirmative action.

Ultimately, it took a masterful speech by President

Clinton, at the United States Archives ("within these walls are America's bedrocks of our common ground— the Declaration of Independence, the Constitution, the Bill of Rights"), in which he announced his policy of "Mend It, Don't End It" and called for a case-by-case review of federal affirmative action programs, to help quell the fire. But the challenges to the policy will undoubtedly continue.

The Supreme Court also dealt a grievous blow to majority black and Latino voting districts that have fostered the political empowerment of African Americans at the state and federal levels. This is yet another example of America's shifting social paradigm. The strength of the Congressional Black Caucus is a barometer of the voting strength of African Americans. Black political power reached its zenith in 1993–94, before the 1994 elections, in part, because of the increase in African American representation in the House of Representatives after the 1992 election, from 23 to 38 voting members. The increased political strength of African Americans at the national level was felt immediately.

As Elaine Jones, director and counsel of the NAACP Legal Defense and Educational Fund, pointed out, for example, white members of the House voted against banning assault weapons by a margin of 212 to 180, and Southern whites voted against the ban 89 to 49. The prohibition passed the House only because 36 of 38 African American representatives voted for it. Similarly, President Clinton's federal budget was rejected by a majority of white Southerners in the House, but was passed 219 to 213, thanks only to the votes of all 17 Southern African American representatives. The 1994 election changed all that. Republicans are in control of Congress, and the attack on majority black voting districts only adds to the despair.

The threats facing African Americans seemed to make President Clinton's reelection imperative. His reelection seemed to be so imperative that when the president signed the welfare bill, many African American leaders were reluctant to criticize him out of fear that such criticisms would deter African Americans from voting in the 1996 presidential election. On the other hand, the signing of the bill was a calculated move to the center and indicated the president's willingness to sacrifice the poor and already disenfranchised. The unfair use of African Americans as the symbol of the welfare poor to spur the end of welfare "as we know it" is only the most recent example of the intentional marginalization of the African American population. In the minds of most politicians, the votes of African Americans are either taken for granted or no great loss.

THE CHANGING ECONOMIC ORDER

Among the factors that contribute to the uncertain future of African Americans is America's economic decline. Assuming that recent rates of immigration will remain constant, it is projected that the foreign-born population of the United States will grow from 19.8 million in 1990 (7.9 percent of the resident population) to 31.1 million in 2010 (10.4 percent), with the number of immigrants from Latin America and Asia increasing the most. Race in America is likely to retain its salience as the proportion of African Americans grows to approximately 15 percent of the population by 2020 and as immigration increases the number and proportion of Asian Americans and Hispanics.

These demographics and the changing economy also have significant implications for the American workforce. It is no secret that the past ten years have been difficult economically for the United States. In its groundbreaking 1987 study, *Workforce 2000*, the Hudson Institute reported that despite its international comeback, U.S. manufacturing will be a much smaller share of the economy in the year 2000 than it is today. Service industries will create all the new jobs and most of the new wealth into the next century. The American workforce will grow slowly over the next few years, becoming older, more female, and more disadvantaged. Only 15 percent of the new workers will be native white men, compared to about 47 percent today. Tensions over the economy and the unavailability of work make it difficult to resolve America's racial problems.

Felix Rohatyn, the New York investment banker, famous as the financial guru who rescued New York City from financial disaster when the city faced bankruptcy in the 1970s, gave a visionary speech at the National Press Club in December 1994 entitled "Advanced Capitalism and the New Politics." He opened with a strong argument in favor of political bipartisanship, a formula that, together with the cooperation of business and labor, enabled the New York City bailout to work and to usher in a decade of prosperity. Political bipartisanship is the foundation of the progressive civil and human rights coalition of the past and will be a key element in any future strategy to address the nation's most intractable problems.

Rohatyn made the point that "advanced capitalism," which he described as a twenty-first-century, market-driven phenomenon that disregards the importance of human capital, was creating its own political realities globally, and that time was not on the side of those who would avoid its worst effects. He also listed the contradictions of the American economy: several years of sustained economic growth, millions of new jobs, low inflation, and rising financial markets and the simultaneous firing of millions of workers by companies that are restructuring, while technology and competition have kept average incomes from rising. The big beneficiaries of this expansion have been owners of financial assets and a new class of highly compensated technicians who are working for companies in which profit sharing and stock ownership were widely spread. The losers were workers who were formerly tied to manufacturing companies, now victimized by progress and global competition, but who are also experiencing the unsettling effects of the profound changes—a combination of fear of the future and cynicism about the present.

The pressures in a representative democracy like ours are enormous, as economic uncertainty tears at the innate sense of societal well-being and combines with a deep-seated hostility for the country's ongoing failure to address long-standing social problems. This anxiety is present notwithstanding the veneer of national economic vitality, and it contributes to political and social instability. The emergence of gang-controlled, drug-economy subcultures in the inner cities; the phenomenon of the so-called angry white male in the 1994 election; and the rise of the militia movement are manifestations of these problems.

The isolation of inner cities over the past two decades has been devastating. Although inner-city children need the most help, they attend the least adequate schools and live in the most dangerous neighborhoods, thanks, in part, to the ready availability of high-powered firearms, the narrowest and most impoverished job market, and the most limited and tenuous understanding of what it takes to make it in the outside world. Residential racial segregation has been identified as the principal structural factor of American society that is responsible for the persistence of urban poverty and the major cause of racial inequality in the United States.

These problems cannot be changed by short-term

income distribution alone. They can be changed by governmental policies that encourage savings and business investment and provide a level of public investment appropriate for the twenty-first century's technology- and information-based society. The business community must recognize the links among private investment, national stability, and confidence in the future. The business community must also encourage the government to establish policies that are responsive to this reality, recognizing that, for the foreseeable future, a large number of Americans will be out of work and will require assistance to enter new career paths. Given the shifts in political power in this country, the business community can play a vital role in seeing to it than an appropriate role for the government is maintained.

How can we as a society address these unresolved problems? How can we tackle the challenges ahead? What steps are needed to move America from a state of denial to a state of grace? The search for solutions must begin with a level of honesty that may be unpleasant, but necessary, if the country is to move forward. I am reminded of President Clinton's speech in October 1995 on race relations in which he said: "White Americans and black Americans often see the same world in drastically different ways. . . . The rift we see before us that is tearing at the heart of America . . . [is] rooted in the awful history and stubborn persistence of racism . . . in the different ways we experience the threats of modern life . . . in the fact that we still haven't learned to talk frankly, to listen carefully, and to work together across racial lines."

Race relations have undergone fundamental changes over the past forty years. However, a new set of obstacles has emerged from inadequate solutions to the old problems of housing discrimination and racial isolation in public schools, as well as structural changes in the economy that may prove more daunting to correct than the original problems of racial segregation of the modern civil rights movement.

Prolonged, high levels of unemployment in the black community, coupled with massive "downsizing" (layoffs) among all workers, have created a level of marginality that negatively affects the poor, regardless of race. The conditions of underclass whites, Hispanics, Asian Americans, and Native Americans reflect, to a greater or lesser degree, the effects of advanced capitalism.

It cannot be overstated how the continuing segregation of our schools contributes to and exacerbates our racial divide. We must finally make a commitment to end de facto segregation and improve public education in Grades K through 12, with an emphasis on establishing high-quality and universal standards. Perhaps the most direct route to ending segregated schooling is to create truly fair housing opportunities. Housing controls individuals' access to high-quality public education, viable employment opportunities, and diverse neighborhoods; thus, persons who experience housing discrimination are not only robbed of their choice of where it is best for them and their families to live, but are effectively denied their very right to pursue the American Dream. Only by investments in urban centers through public and private partnerships, the rehabilitation of public housing, and the creation of state and federal jobs programs will we be able to give our working class the means with which they can contribute to society. The new welfare reform legislation places a premium on the creation of jobs only at the bottom of the wage scale—jobs that are viable for no one.

Increasing the number of voters is a key to fostering feelings of commitment to the present democratic system and an understanding that those in office are beholden to those who vote for them and are hurt by those who vote against them. Historic appeals to young people, many of whom were born after the height of the modern civil rights movement, no longer prove effective. Their rational self-interest must be addressed before young people can see themselves as having a stake in the process. In addition, civic education must again become part of the public education curriculum and must be provided as well by civic, fraternal, and religious organizations.

We also must mount an aggressive attack to reduce the level of hate crimes and violence in American society. The increase in hate crimes across a broad spectrum of citizens is troubling. It is symptomatic of a larger national problem that cries out for attention.

Most important, the Darden Dilemma cannot be resolved by denying social injustice or by separatist solutions that are disconnected from the struggles of other subordinated people for inclusion. The African American middle class must strive mightily to find ways to reach across the class divide in our community and the racial divide that besets the nation. Pretending that all is right with America because a few African Americans have managed to break through is no solution. Working to make things right is.

Wade Henderson is the executive director of the Leadership Conference on Civil Rights, an organization established in 1950 to promote the passage and implementation of civil rights laws. He was formerly the Washington Bureau director of the National Association for the Advancement of Colored People, where he was in charge of governmental affairs and the NAACP's national legislative program. He began his career working for the American Civil Liberties Union, where he rose to the position of associate director of the national office in Washington. He is the author of numerous articles on civil rights and public policy issues.

From James Madison to Christopher Darden:

The American Struggle for Truth and Order

ROGER WILKINS

As a black prosecutor, Christopher Darden had a tough job in a rough town. And then things got worse. He drew a rotten case and got famous in an ugly way. The office he worked for didn't seem to be supremely competent, and the police department that did the investigation had, over the years, developed a reputation for racism and brutality. Then it turned out that the police department wasn't competent in conducting high-profile investigations either. Race was a powerful factor in the case, and Darden was on the wrong side of black public opinion. It was pretty awful for him, but, in my judgment, he was in the right place at the right time.

I now have to make a couple of confessions. I am a black man who concluded that O. J. Simpson murdered

Nicole Brown Simpson and Ronald Goldman even before the great Bronco chase. The farewell note did it for me. I reasoned this way: Had I been innocent and writing a note as the police were on their way to arrest me, the words, "I did not kill my wife" would have been very high up in the text. I surely wouldn't have written a maudlin set of farewells to all and sundry. My mind would have been on an all-out fight for acquittal that would surely have involved everybody close to me. So why say good-bye?

Nevertheless, to my everlasting embarrassment, when the trial actually got under way, a large part of me looked at Darden with disdain. I thoughtlessly assumed that he was a black-skinned prop, deployed by the Los Angeles criminal justice system as a decoy for fairness. Simply because of his race and his employment (as I indicate later, I have reason for my special feelings about Los Angeles justice), I had leaped to a sloppy and utterly unsupported denial of the truth and the complexity of Darden's humanity. As a black person and one who is supposed to know how to think, a former official of the Department of Justice and a teacher of history, I should have known better.

But whether Darden conducted himself effectively during the trial or appropriately afterward is beyond my interest here. Rather, given the complexity of the issues concerning the intersection of race and justice in this case, the more important questions this trial inspired have to do with the general state of black-white relations in the United States, seen first through the prism of blacks working in the law-and-order system. The Simpson trial aside, criminal justice is the place to begin any discussion of race in this country because the seeds of many of the problems that plague us today were planted when the American justice system was being created.

Our system of criminal justice generally rests on principles of truth and order. No society can function adequately without some semblance of order that lends a measure of safety and predictability to daily life. In the United States, we seek to limit the means of achieving that order by observing a truth about ourselves and each other that we agreed on at the founding of the Republic and to which we have given general assent through the twenty-two decades of the life of the nation. That truth is stated in what must be the most famous sentence ever written by an American: "We hold these truths to be self-evident, that all men are created equal, that they are endowed by their Creator with certain unalienable rights, that among these are life, liberty and the pursuit of happiness."

The American colonies rebelled in an effort to achieve a society that was ordered in a way that suited them much better than the one decreed by King George III and his council. One of the principal elements of that new order was the acceptance as civic truth of the idea that each human being has an essential dignity that must be respected and is thus entitled to a cluster of rights to protect that dignity against the depredations of the state. If it worked appropriately, then the criminal justice system might be seen as a truth, order, and justice system.

But the intersection of order and truth in the American system of criminal justice has always been an explosive place when race is dropped into the mix. To complicate matters further, the attitudes toward the innate rights of African Americans by those in power have always been ambivalent. In the beginning, there was a yearning among many Americans—even among many slave owners—for at least a modicum of civic decency. But this yearning was rather fainthearted, and it competed for space in American culture with violence and hypocrisy. Today we have achieved immeasurably more decency, but there still is far more ambivalence, violence, and hypocrisy than is good for the health and the future of this nation.

Our laws, including those that Darden was sworn to uphold, reflect the nation's economic structures and its cultural realities. While this is, indeed, a multicultural society, whites peopled it in superior numbers and conquered or suppressed others with violence and guile and then with economic and police power. As conquerors, they imposed cultural and economic orders that reflected their victories. They composed the stories about how progress was made; they assigned the human weight to be given to various groups of human beings and made up the cultural "truths" about these groups. The legal system codifies many of these schemes. With respect to blacks, the schemes have been particularly ugly. To comprehend the issues of race and justice that plague today's society, it is essential to understand the full force of our historically prejudiced judicial system.

After a brief period of indentured servitude, blacks were reduced, by the middle of the seventeenth century, to a state of perpetual, hereditary slavery. Virtually any level of sophistry or degree of violence against black people was permitted to perpetuate this order. Laws were drafted and court decisions were rendered to ensure the entrenchment of this arrangement. And the laws were clear, with the conceptual foundations of blacks' inferior status laid out in the Constitution. In the *Federalist Papers* No. 54, James Madison wrote that black humanity was "divested of two fifths of the man," by way of justifying the compromise permitting slaves to be counted as three-fifths of a person for the purpose of apportioning seats in the House of Representatives.

Legally sanctioned violence undergirded this system of racial order. In *In the Matter of Color: Race and the American Legal Process: The Colonial Period*, A. Leon Higginbotham, the former chief judge of the U.S. Court of Appeals for the Third Circuit, described a nineteenth-century North Carolina case, *State v. Mann*, in which the rationale supporting this violence was laid bare. The case arose when charges of criminal battery were brought against a white for an assault upon a female slave. According to Higginbotham, the court said that "a slave was to 'labor upon a principle of natural duty,' to disregard 'his own personal happiness,' and that the purpose of the legal system was to convince each slave that he had 'no will of his own [and that he must surrender] his will in implicit obedience to that of another. Such obedience is the consequence only of uncontrolled authority over the body. There is nothing else that can operate to produce the effect. The power of the master must be absolute to render the submission of the slave perfect.'"

A few years after the North Carolina Supreme Court handed down that decision, Chief Justice Roger Taney faced similar issues in *Dred Scott v. Sanford*. Scott, a slave, was suing for his freedom on the grounds that he became free when his master had taken him into a free state. In his opinion for the Supreme Court, Taney probed the intentions of the Founding Fathers at the time of the Declaration of Independence concerning the rights of blacks and concluded: "The unhappy black race were separated from the white by indelible marks, and laws long before established, and were never thought of or spoken of except as property. . . . [Blacks were] beings of an inferior order, and altogether unfit to associate with the white race, either in social or political relations; and so far inferior that they had no rights which the white man was bound to respect."

The foregoing aspects of American law constitute elements of the psychic sovereignty that whites imposed on the nation and that pushed blacks to the very margins of human existence and to the bottom of the national structure of respect. Whites were powerful enough to shape the culture, to define truth and ownership in virtually all spheres of human existence, to regulate behavior, and even to shape psychic reactions to social stimuli. For now it is sufficient to say that in predominantly white institutions, psychic sovereignty means that the ways of understanding things, performing work, and conducting oneself in public are all controlled or at least dominated by white understandings and white patterns of behavior.

Buried under all this or at least brutalized by it are some "self-evident truths" about blacks. We are, and have always been, human beings who are capable of love and foolishness and thought and evil and loyalty and ignorance and creativity and self-delusion, just as whites or anybody else are. But the American system of order, shrouded in pretensions of rationality, from earliest times constructed a new truth in which blacks were diminished to fantasies that were useful to whites for perpetuating the order in which they possessed almost the total array of power and privilege in the society. This new construction, of course, involved the simultaneous persistent and comprehensive inflation of the whites' psychic sense of themselves. Thus, the order-keeping system was not built on a decent understanding of human truth, but, rather—as Chief Justice Taney demonstrated—on a set of Founding Fantasies.

This system of truth did perpetuate an order of sorts. Rich and powerful whites were on top. Blacks were excluded altogether. And the loyalty of poor whites to the system was bought with their status as nonblacks, which allowed them to be members of the white club and thus privy to a sense of entitlement, superiority, and dreams of limitless possibility.

Of course, an order based on such flawed premises carried enormous costs. Among them were that it placed violence close to the core of the national project and caused terrible turmoil in the souls of those it ensnared. From the beginning, slave owners were obsessed to the point of paranoia with the possibility that the slaves might revolt or that an individual slave might inflict dreadful harm on them. This obsession accounted, in large measure, for the brutality in the reasoning in *State v. Mann*. Thus, the violence employed to subordinate blacks led to an obsession with the need to husband reserve capacities of violence in case violence was needed to deal with the dangers that violent racial subordination had created.

It goes without saying that the laws developed under slavery provided neither truth nor order for blacks. There could be no orderly arrangements between husband and wife that did not hang under the cloud of some arbitrary step the master might take. Similarly, there could be no orderly arrangements between parent and child or, indeed, between the slave and his or her own soul. Raw power controlled the daily lives of the slaves, and psychological domination wreaked havoc with the inner lives of large numbers of them. In its essence, slavery was the very antithesis of both truth and order.

Life after slavery left many things unchanged. The former slave owners were so intent on retaining the economic, social, psychological, and sexual advantages of the old system that (with the complicity of powerful Northerners) they soon made new laws and invented new forms of violence to continue America as they had known it. Ultimately, custom overwhelmed the fine post–Civil War intentions written into the Constitution as men clothed in constitutional authority and black robes enshrined racist fantasies, such as *Plessy v. Ferguson*, into constitutional doctrine.

The degradation of black life by the terrorists of the Ku Klux Klan and spontaneous mobs, legislators, police officials, and judges—particularly in the South, but in other parts of the country as well—continued to drive white privilege and black subordination deep into both the cultural and legal practices of America. Burnished, modified, and elaborated through the generations, the deep cultural and resulting legal structures of white domination became behavioral and psychological hallmarks of what America actually was. During those days, blacks were almost entirely excluded from administering the formal processes of the criminal justice system (which, when it came to blacks, might better have been called the truth-denying, order-keeping system).

Cultural habits die hard. Today blacks do participate in the order-keeping system, but unacceptable levels of ambivalence, violence, and hypocrisy remain. As of this writing, for example, New York authorities are investigating the killing in a subway station of an unarmed black man, Nathaniel Levi Gaines Jr., by a white policeman. Though no charges had ever been levied against Gaines, after his death by bullet wounds to his back, investigators turned up at his place of work trying to "dig up some dirt," according to Bob Herbert in the *New York Times.*

The officer who shot Gaines, Paolo Colecchia, had previously been implicated in three race-tinged incidents in which the use of excessive force was alleged. Despite all his problems, Colecchia was still permitted to perform as an order-keeping instrument. Mayor Rudolph Giuliani said "[T]here does not appear to be an explanation for [the shooting]." Mr. Gaines's father told Bob Herbert: "We didn't want to say that his life was taken because he was born with his skin dark. But there is no other explanation."

Even so, there is far more truth in the criminal order system today than there was fifty years ago, and that is, in large measure, a result of the introduction of a significant number of minorities as workers in the field. Thurgood Marshall and his allies struggled for years to achieve such inclusion because they realized just how dangerous and damaging the absence had always been.

And so we have circled back to Darden's burden.

There is no more important concept in American criminal law than the presumption of innocence. It is a powerful attempt to guarantee the right of the lone individual against the awesome power of the state. It is also an attempt to guarantee that each person who is caught up in the system will be treated as an individual.

Unfortunately, it still doesn't always work. In some places, poor, alienated black men are *presumed guilty*, not because of who they are as individuals, but because of where they are from, what they look like, and what their cultural affect is. In too many big cities, criminal justice is an ugly business. It is often carried on in battered courtrooms by overburdened and harried people, from judges to prosecutors to underpaid defense lawyers to police officers to bailiffs and jailers. However we Americans may have viewed the "refuse of [somebody else's] teeming shore," the refuse of America's poorest streets doesn't look attractive to these overburdened people. The task of sorting out the individuality of surly, beaten, often defiant (and often guilty) people is sometimes beyond the capacities of the workers in this strained system.

Darden's burden, in addition to the responsibility of doing his job as professionally as possible, was to dent the psychic sovereignty encountered in such places with the human truth of black life and of individual black lives. The task is to turn the order-keeping process into a truth and order process. People in his shoes often have to teach those truths against the grain of the institutional culture of their place of employment and sometimes are treated as the enemy within. They also have to teach that blacks abhor lawlessness and are prepared to prosecute and incarcerate black as well as white criminals.

However difficult that burden is inside the institution, its weight is increased enormously by the black cultural memory of the order-keeping process as a principal instrument of racial subordination and of the complicity of so many blacks in it. Power often works hard to corrupt and to co-opt. The history of using blacks against other blacks has deep roots in slavery. There were brutal black overseers. There were also black informers. Plans for slave insurrections and escapes were often betrayed by other slaves who were seeking the masters' favor. In later generations, some blacks in law enforcement played out those roles, having concluded that they were accountable only to white power. Blacks working in the order-keeping system today carry the burden of that history, as my instinctive reaction to Darden illustrates. Again, I should have known better.

As director of the Community Relations Service in the Department of Justice from 1966 to 1969 and as associate director for the eighteen months preceding that period, I participated in one of the most important American systems of order. Much of our work in those days dealt with what most people called riots and what many blacks called urban rebellions. Although hoodlums were certainly involved in much of the looting and burning, I saw the rebellions essentially as cries of rage and desperation from a people long ignored and despised. While restoration of order was obviously the first priority, the revelation of a deep social truth as a first step toward establishing greater justice was the central aim and overall goal of our program.

Those of us who cared about this work were deeply seared by the distance between the needs of the excluded and defamed people whose lives we were trying to present truthfully to the world, on the one hand, and the capacities of the institutions for which we worked, on the other hand. One aspect of the government's lack of capacity was, of course, that its values and perceptions were basically those of middle- to upper-class whites, tinged with that little extra spice of arrogance that comes with power. Not all our white colleagues fit this description, but enough did to make the work difficult and sometimes heartbreaking.

Few experiences in my governmental career better demonstrated the conflicting pressures and pulls of the role of black governmental officials in the truth-and-order tug-of-war than my two weeks in Los Angeles during and after the Watts riot in 1965. Watts was the first place where there was burning as well as looting and where television covered the frightening events live and in color. It was the place where the hideous combination of human urban misery and public and private indifference, neglect, and incapacity were on display for all who wanted to see. I was sent by President Lyndon Johnson to assist, first, Commerce Undersecretary LeRoy Collins and, later, Deputy Attorney General Ramsey Clark, who were to help restore order and to rationalize federal assistance to the community.

It quickly became apparent to me that it was essential for those important white federal officials to be exposed to black people who were not in the thin top level of local black leadership with whom the civic leaders of Los Angeles were used to dealing. The conventional black leaders led fairly protected middle-class lives, cushioned from the harsh realities that people in South Central Los Angeles or Watts had to face. The black director of the Los Angeles Human Relations Commission, for example, told me that he had not been in Watts for the whole decade preceding the riot. Consequently, I arranged a meeting so that Collins and I could meet some of the residents of Watts to get a clear sense of them as individuals and of their lives as *they* experienced them.

Collins's charter was simply to put together agreements among the local political powers that would enable funds to begin to trickle in from the new fledgling antipoverty programs. He controlled no program funds that he could dispense. But to the people we were visiting, such fine distinctions had no meaning. Collins was in their sights, and they were furious at whites, in general, and at this symbol of white authority and his black assistant, in particular.

For two hours, Collins and I stood together in front of people boiling with hurt and rage. We absorbed a fierce and ceaseless assault on the malfeasance of society and our own presumed complicity in every deprivation and indignity in their daily lives. We learned, for example, that job networks did not extend to Watts. We learned that elderly people had to ride buses and transfer two or three times to get to social security and public health facilities. We learned that virtually any contact with people in authority elicited rudeness and that when the contact was with the Los Angeles Police Department, there was frequently unprovoked official violence. And finally, of course, we learned that the real rates of unemployment in these communities ranged up to 50 percent. In response to all these complaints, Collins tried to explain how limited his charter and his power were. An angry woman screamed at him, calling him a liar, and told him to get out of there and to take his "little yella Uncle Tom" with him.

Nevertheless, our firsthand knowledge of the texture of the deprivations in these communities eased our task of putting together the agreements that would enable the poverty money to begin to flow into the community. Though we knew the amounts available would be minuscule compared to the monumental needs to which we had been exposed, we consoled ourselves with the thought that it was "a start." We knew, however, that the start was pitiful and were both deeply pained that our national understanding and our national will were so severely and racially constricted.

Near the end of the assignment, a white colleague from the Commerce Department and I were pulled over by two white police officers just after we had turned off Wilshire Boulevard to go to our hotel. Though my colleague, who had been driving (and was dressed as I was, in a suit and tie) had broken no traffic laws, we were ordered out of the car at gunpoint. The officer who interrogated me was tight with anger. After I showed him two pieces of governmental identification, both of which had photographs of me and described me accurately, I refused his demand that I produce my driver's license.

"You saw that I wasn't driving," I said, "and you have two laminated cards that identify me as a U.S. government employee and we weren't breaking any laws— unless it's against the law for a Negro guy and a white guy to ride together in a car in L.A."

With this impertinence, the man's whole body, including the hand in which he held the gun, began to shake.

"Well, I work for a government, too. Show me your driver's license now!" he commanded. His gun moved a little bit. At that moment, I realized that my insistence on a bit of dignity had profoundly challenged the racial fantasies of an armed white man who was clothed in authority and that my life might end right there. Generations of American culture had given this man an almost reflexive response to blacks who exhibited a will of their own.

Fortunately, at that moment, the other officer, having learned from his calmer interrogation of my colleague what a colossal mistake they had made, came over to the gun-wielding officer and said jovially:

"Boy, have we made a mistake! Do you know who we have here?"

"I don't give a damn!" the officer hissed, his gun never wavering and his eyes blazing hatred. But finally, his partner walked him away and talked him down a bit. And our encounter with our local colleagues in the order-keeping business was over.

Life for blacks in institutions that are not specifically devoted to order and justice, though not as acutely painful, often poses similar psychological difficulties. I pass by the enormous problems of attempting to compete inside an institution with people who have networks and mentors when you have none and the predictable tendency of such organizations to shunt blacks into soft staff roles, rather than put them in the line of ascendancy that leads to the top. It is the twin issues of psychic sovereignty and truth-telling that concern me here.

When I speak of psychic sovereignty in the late-twentieth-century context, I am speaking of something that is a cultural remnant of the early days of the Republic. It is obviously less comprehensive and brutal than that described by Chief Justice Taney or the North Carolina court in the *Mann* case. But it does include a fairly strong sense—on the part of many whites—that the prevailing white cultural understanding of blacks is uncontrovertible truth. It also includes an enormous element of denial directed back to our past and to the tight hold on all our psyches that our cultural history still exerts.

In my view, contemporary psychic sovereignty also includes the sometimes subconscious sense that most whites seem to have that America is a white country. These whites surely have created for themselves a psychic ease that blacks and others do not share. For example, most whites can go into any restaurant anywhere in the nation, whether it's just off Park Avenue in New York City or is some rough, rural beer-and-sandwich stand in Appalachia, without worrying much about how they will be received. Few blacks would do so without a wary eye out for, at the least, discourtesy and, at the worst, real danger.

The contrast between the attitudes of white and black college students on predominantly white campuses is instructive. In the spring and fall, when the weather is good, white students put on their shorts, take out their footballs and Frisbees, and play or sprawl all over every available piece of attractive campus real estate. They don't exhibit a bit of doubt that this is *their* place to use however they choose. The black experience, on the contrary, was described to me by a student in Oklahoma:

"They look at me like, 'What are you doing here?'"

"When do they look at you like that, Oscar?" I asked.

"Every time I walk in a door," he replied.

Affluent adult blacks have had exactly the same experience when we trespass across a line that the conventional psychic sovereignty has drawn as the border between what belongs to whites and that area across the line called "blacks' place" (as in "He knows his place" or "Why don't they stay in their place?"). Resorts where blacks are rarely seen or upscale restaurants in remote spots will elicit some of the rudest stares imaginable. And when a black man is with a white woman, the looks can turn from rude to withering.

Perhaps the strongest current institutional examples of psychic sovereignty occur in news organizations. Whites are so used to defining truth, deciding what is important and what is not and judging who is worth listening to and who and what ideas are insignificant and are so profoundly comfortable inside the general white understanding of things that blacks have a hard time bringing their point of view into print or onto the screen.

A striking example of this phenomenon occurred in the *New York Times* newsroom when I worked there a few years ago. After work one day, several black writers and reporters happened to come together and were engaged in a casual conversation when the then-editor of the *New York Times Magazine* approached us. After looking past us toward rows of empty desks, he said idly: "I came down looking for some writers, but I guess they've all gone home."

In the complex world of the 1990s, the racial road map is difficult to navigate. The minds and spirits of white Americans have traveled an enormous distance since the early part of this century. Whites can contemplate the possibility of a Colin Powell presidency with equanimity. They can make Michael Jordan, Oprah Winfrey, and Denzel Washington fabulously rich with no apparent envy or resentment. Middle-class blacks have trouble slogging through institutional trenches up to the higher reaches, whether of law firms, newspapers, or auto manufacturers. But we are now granted a substantial amount of psychic space in most urban settings.

It is the realm of economic and political truth where the largest problems arise. After opening up to blacks in general in the 1960s, public and political opinion began to close down hard on the black poor—and on people who attempted to speak for them—during the 1970s. That hardening has continued through the last decade and a half. The process began in response to civil rights legislation and to the urban riots of the late 1960s and picked up steam as politicians began to scratch at the old racist cultural itch.

Former Alabama Governor George Wallace came to the North in his 1968 and 1972 campaigns and taught Northern politicians how to repackage some of the old racist politics of the South. He talked about "pointy-headed Federal bureaucrats" who thought they knew how to run peoples' lives better than the people themselves did. At the same time, Richard Nixon was running a campaign that called for "law and order." Against the background of the riots and federal efforts to enforce desegregation, these messages were enormously powerful. They combined racism (tinged strongly by fears of black violence) with the traditional American distrust of an active government.

This new politics gathered momentum in the mid-1970s, when the economic booms of post–World War II and the Vietnam War began to fade and many families found themselves either working harder just to stay in place or falling further and further behind. Somebody or something had to be to blame. The Great Society's coddling of the frightening and shiftless black poor became the answer of choice that conservative politicians began serving to the American people as a regular diet.

These messages gain their resonance from behavior in the poorest black precincts that most Americans find deeply troubling. We are fed a steady diet on nighttime local news programs of crime and dissolution in ghetto neighborhoods, and the popular culture is filled with tales of single black teenage mothers and irresponsible fathers. Understandings of this behavior, for the conventional white mind, are supplied, in the first instance, not by the mass media or by politicians, but by white attitudes toward blacks that have rumbled down through the centuries.

Understanding our national culture, conservatives

began to present the Republican Party as the party of white people and law and order and the Democratic Party as the party of "special interests," minorities and coddlers of criminals. In the wake of the devastatingly effective Willie Horton ad used by George Bush in his 1988 campaign, Democrats became more conservative and were intent on showing the country that they could "handle" their minorities. The general consensus formed by white opinion makers and journalists moved significantly to the right as well.

The psychic sovereignty of the 1990s is, more than anything, tightly focused on the black poor. Crime and welfare have been the hottest domestic-policy topics of the decade, and the discussions proceed as if there are no whites on welfare and little white crime to be concerned about.

Fantasies and denials that carry hints of the Founding Fantasies supply gross conventional understandings about America's most vulnerable people. A major element of the denial brushes aside the cultural weight of this country's three-hundred-year history of doing damage to the black poor. There are also denials about the damage done to poor blacks by twenty-three straight years of double-digit unemployment and the fact that such unemployment produces similar behavior in other populations, no matter what their color. Though few would now argue that blacks are only worth three-fifths of whites, there is more than an echo of that fantasy in the popularity of such books as *The Bell Curve*. The fantasy is also evident in the political idea that welfare and the Great Society, rather than depression-like levels of joblessness, are the principal reasons for undesirable behavior in poor black precincts. Seeds left by the Founding Fantasies can surely be seen in the conviction that the behavioral problems of the black poor can best be treated by either vigorous criminal prosecution or by punitive social policies.

Finally, in a massive summary denial of history and common sense, conventional wisdom suggests that the civil rights movement and responses to it took care of the cumulative damage done to blacks over centuries and that now racially targeted remedies are the true barriers to achieving our goal of a color-blind society.

The result is that the outline of today's version of white psychic sovereignty is almost as hard as that under which blacks suffered early in the century, when we were simply deemed too inferior for integration to be considered. This is not to assert that America today is as harsh as it was sixty years ago, but to suggest that the currently perceived truths on race are as difficult to crack today as were those of the 1930s. Whites are deeply worried about order, among other things, and have developed a set of targeted fantasies that give them comfort and about which they are not prepared to entertain any debate.

A famous white journalist—who was then employed by *two* major news organizations—insisted on seeing me not long ago. This man, approximately fifteen years my junior, sat in my living room and proceeded not to interview me, but to tell me what *he* thought about affirmative action. When he was through, I began to tell him what I thought, drawing on a lifetime spent in and around the civil rights movement. I hadn't talked half as long as he had when he burst out, "Bullshit!" So much for my experience and insight. So much for my American truth. He gets paid well and receives a lot of prominence to publish neoconservative ideas that trot along the well-worn path of today's conventional wisdom.

Whites have no idea how infuriating such behavior is, whether it comes from individuals like the *Times* editor or from institutions like the two news organizations that accepted my journalist visitor's perceptions as revealed social truth. Senator Daniel Patrick Moynihan has mused that middle-class blacks have "an exaggerated sense of aggrievement," as if our response to the limited advances in this generation should make us first, grateful, and second, oblivious to the abject plight of so many millions of our fellow blacks. Such foolish and careless observations—offhand applications of psychic sovereignty—simply add to our "sense of aggrievement."

Nevertheless, there is still some good black-white cooperation in this country, and there are a number of forums for dialogue. There are many white professionals in the civil rights movement, and there are concerned whites in progressive political movements as well. Moreover, all over the country, valuable mentoring and community service programs are being carried out by interracial groups. Howard University and the American Jewish Committee just launched a new magazine, *CommonQuest*, that seeks to further black-Jewish understanding, and a number of judges of all races in New York City have come together, calling themselves Blacks and Jews in Conversation, to combat bigotry among young people. Moreover, while I have used the actions of certain "whites" and the impact of "psychic sovereignty" almost interchangeably, I do not intend to suggest that there are not millions of decent, open, and mature white Americans who don't need a racially inflated sense of themselves to cope with life.

All that being said, conventional wisdom still has a rigid hold on the political and journalistic elite who are managers of psychic sovereignty in the 1990s. So, like Darden, a lot of us have a tough job in a rough country. Things are going against us right now. But successful blacks have the wonderful advantage of drawing strength from our black heritage and from the opportunity that we have to tell the truth for people who cannot speak for themselves because of the damage that continues to be done to them.

The heritage is absolutely ennobling. In the decades before the North Carolina court rendered its decision in the *Mann* case, Absalom Jones and Richard Allen—both former slaves—created a black self-help institution in Philadelphia and broke away from the indignities of second-class worship. Allen founded the African Methodist Episcopal Church.

When days were dark, at around the time of the *Dred Scott* case, Harriet Tubman freed herself and then, instead of remaining in safety as a seamstress in Philadelphia, she risked her life by returning time and time again to the South to bring other slaves to freedom. Frederick Douglass thundered against the evils of slavery when even some white abolitionists were insufferably patronizing to him. Strong black people didn't wait for white people to validate them and their truths. They simply acted out their humanity and spoke out their truths. And so it went, down the line from W. E. B. DuBois to Mary McLeod Bethune to Charles Hamilton Houston to Thurgood Marshall to Fannie Lou Hamer and to Martin Luther King Jr.

One does not need to be a hero to participate in this struggle. One day, on my way to work at the *New York Times*, I realized that a black colleague of mine was climbing the subway stairs just in front of me. He was a man who was largely ignored and disrespected inside the paper (once he was leaving a party with a beautiful black woman, and a white *Times* editor looked through him and said to her: "Gee, it's a shame, you're going home alone"), but who had wonderful insights about black life and art. He was sometimes capable of driving his vision through the screens of editorial indifference or outright hostility and into print with striking and elegant effect. He didn't know I was behind him when he got to the top of the stairs, squared his shoulders, and said, mainly, I think, to himself: "Well, here I am again!"

In doing so, he was bringing his truth and his indomitable spirit to the daily struggle. He and millions like him around the country would make a difference that day as they carried on that tradition in the institutions where they worked.

The requirement for blacks these days is, as it always has been, to go back to the fundamental civic truth: that all men and women are created equal and it is therefore incumbent upon us to carry that truth about ourselves and our least fortunate brethren into the world's battles. The psychic sovereignty imposed by white America is not nearly as suffocating now as it has been in centuries past because there were people who did in their time what needed to be done.

We must have faith that our truth-telling struggles will continue to chip away at the Founding Fantasies and that someday a vast majority of whites will be able without fear to face our nation's past, to accept our common humanity and our shared destiny. Then, truth, order, and justice may truly intersect in the United States of America.

Roger Wilkins, a Justice Department official in the Johnson administration and later a journalist with the Washington Post *and the* New York Times, *is now a professor of history at George Mason University.*